NATIONAL GUARD 101:

A Handbook for Spouses

Mary Corbett

Savas Beatie

New York and California

Library of Congress Cataloging-in-Publication Data
Corbett, Mary.
National Guard 101 : a handbook for spouses / Mary Corbett— 2nd ed.
p. cm.
Includes bibliographical references and index.
ISBN 978-1-61121-068-2 (alk. paper)
1. Military spouses—United States—Handbooks, manuals, etc. 2. United States—National Guard—Family relationships. 3. United States. Army—Military life—Handbooks, manuals, etc. 4. Families of military personnel—Services for—United States—Handbooks, manuals, etc. I. Title.
U766.C58 2011b
355.3'70973—dc23
2012035574

18 17 16 15 14   6 5 4 3
Second edition, third printing

SB

Published by
Savas Beatie LLC
989 Governor Drive, Suite 102
El Dorado Hills, CA 95762
Phone: 916-941-6896
Email: sales@savasbeatie.com
Website: www.savasbeatie.com

Savas Beatie titles are available at special discounts for bulk purchases in the United States by corporations, institutions, and other organizations. For more details, please contact Special Sales, P.O. Box 4527, El Dorado Hills, CA 95762, or you may e-mail us at sales@savasbeatie.com, or visit our website at www.savasbeatie.com for additional information.

Dedication

In memory of Lieutenant Nathan A. Nieber of the Minnesota Army National Guard.

Nate was a promising young officer who personified military values and honor.

The youngest commissioned officer in the Army National Guard at the time of his 1998 commissioning, he was an accomplished Infantry officer and graduated first in his class. He was also awarded the William O. Darby Award for displaying the best leadership during Ranger training.

At the time of his death in 2002, he was an active duty member of the 135th Infantry Regiment, 34th Infantry Division, MN ARNG.

Like a lot of Jon's friends, he was a big fan of Robert Heinlein's "Starship Troopers." So in Nate's honor, here is a Heinlein quote that the readers of this book will appreciate:

"You can have peace, or you can have freedom.
Don't ever count on having both at once."

Table of Contents

Preface

My first exposure to the military came with my first job. I worked as a secretary at the advertising firm Young & Rubicam in a group that handled the U.S. Army account. It was all very confusing. There was the active Army, the Army Reserve, and the National Guard. Be All You Can Be, money for college, one weekend a month, two weeks in the summer. It was hard to keep track of who was who and what was what. Besides, I was young! I was in New York! I was much more interested in the hip guys making storyboards in the creative department than the high-speed Army Officers who came for meetings.

I guess the old saying is true: with age comes wisdom. Ten years later, I met a man in uniform and HOOAH! Every brooding artist quickly faded to the background. Our courtship was swift and I was surprised to find out that my fiancé was an Officer in the Minnesota Army National Guard. I thought it was really cool . . . at first. But it didn't take long to realize that there was a lot more to supporting Jon than admiring him in his dress blues. I remember asking Jon if he could just blow off his weekend drill at Camp Ripley. He told me that he could . . . if he wanted to get arrested.

Hmm. Obviously he had signed on to *something*. But just what exactly had I signed on for?

The first time I attended a Guard family event, I felt like I had been abducted by aliens. I didn't understand *anything*. Not one thing. I had never been in an armory before. I didn't know the difference between an officer and enlisted soldier. I didn't know how to address the commander or his wife. Until I met my husband, I didn't know any members of the National Guard (instead of "Guard members," by the way, I'll use "Guardsman" for both male and female National Guard Soldiers) in my acquaintance. Now I knew dozens of Soldiers including the handsome Officers who formed the saber arch at our wedding. During the first two years of our marriage, I did the best I could to support Jon's military career (translation: I pretty much winged it). I showed up where I was supposed to show up, recorded drill dates on the calendar, offered my two cents worth of advice on weekend drill politics and grumbled as he headed off for his two week AT, whatever that meant (my first lesson: Annual Training).

For the most part, except for the annoying inconvenience of drill weekends, my life was untouched and so was my heart. I'll take a pass on the flag pin, thank you very much. I mean, since Jon was "just a Guardsman," I didn't consider myself a *real* military wife. Military spouses lived on bases. Military spouses lived their lives within a strict structure of rank. Military spouses had to deal with deployments. Thank goodness I didn't have to worry about those things. Of course, I could have never guessed, and neither could anyone else, that in less than two years four hijacked airliners would forever alter the purpose and public profile of National Guard Soldiers and those who love them. On September 11, 2001, I became a military wife. But, as I realized later, I had always been one.

That terrible morning, Jon and I were both home awaiting the arrival of our first baby. When Jon called me downstairs, I heard something in his voice that didn't sound right. He told me about the first airplane. We sat in our living room, stunned as we watched the horrors unfold live on our television set. It was too much to comprehend. We had just relocated from Minnesota to Georgia and Jon had yet to attend his first drill with his new battalion. But we both knew that the National Guard would be called to duty immediately.

And it was. Six minutes after the FAA issued its first alert to the 1st Air Force Air Combat Command about a possible hijacking, F-15 fighters from the Massachusetts Air National Guard's 102nd Fighter Wing became the nation's first airborne responder to the terrorist attacks. Soon after, the North Dakota Air National Guard's 119th Fighter Wing, which happened to be at Langley Air Force Base in Virginia, were the first F-16 fighters airborne. Among the people who lost their lives at the Pentagon on September 11 were Active Guard Reserve members Lieutenant Colonel Canfield Boone (Indiana) and Chief Warrant Officer 4 William Ruth (Maryland).

Members of the New York National Guard headed for their armories or the burning towers within minutes of the attack. By the next day, more than 1,200 New York Army National Guard and Air National Guard personnel were on duty. About 500 served near the towers helping police maintain security. In our home state of Georgia, and in most other states, the National Guard immediately moved to secure Army Guard facilities. The Virginia and Maryland National Guards sent Military Police units to help secure the Pentagon.

There is something so profound about volunteer Soldiers from different states coming together so quickly and seamlessly to defend their country. Watching Soldiers and Airmen "come out of nowhere" on September 11th reinforced that we are truly United States. I've never felt so proud of my country or my military.

Our daughter was born on September 14. By then, the shock had worn off a little bit. My sadness was replaced by anger. Rage, really. I felt like we had been sucker-punched and I wanted to hit back. I think most people felt the same way. The country was united. Flag sales skyrocketed. Flag images were displayed on clothing, homes, and vehicles. I noticed a determination in people's eyes. Americans were mad—really mad–and I knew the National Guard would be a part of setting things straight.

On September 20, President Bush addressed a joint session of Congress and the nation. His words foreshadowed a new kind of military operation: "Americans should not expect one battle, but a lengthy campaign, unlike any other we have ever seen. It may include dramatic strikes, visible on TV, and covert operations, secret even in success . . . Every nation, in every region, now has a decision to make. Either you are with us, or you are with the terrorists."

A week later, at his direction, about 5,000 National Guard members were called up to help provide additional security at 422 commercial airports nationwide for four to six months. The national crisis took on local meaning. For me, this was the first time since 9/11 that I felt secure. I also felt proud. Anybody who passed one of our troops in an airport could see their resolve. Their presence sent a message: Nobody is going to keep us down.

Operation Enduring Freedom, the invasion of Afghanistan, began on October 7th. Air National Guard fighters, in air refuelers, and transport aircraft played significant roles in the earliest days of the campaign, well before National Guard troops were on the ground. As the campaign progressed, National Guard troops arrived to help organize and train the Afghan Army. Others took on active combat missions.

In early 2002, like many of his fellow Soldiers, Jon received orders to deploy for Operation Enduring Freedom. He would train at Fort Benning for three months and be stationed at Guantanamo Bay, Cuba, for six months. I was stunned at the speed of the deployment process. He gave his brand-new civilian job immediate notice, started driving to his armory daily, and the rest was a blur. While he was deployed, I was left behind with a six-month-old baby and a full-time job. We were new to the Georgia Guard and lived more than an hour away from his home base armory. I had enough on my plate and getting involved with the Guard's Family Readiness Group wasn't an option. Through divine intervention (or just plain luck), I met a co-worker who was also married to a Guardsman. We immediately bonded. Lynn and Steve were my salvation while Jon was gone. For the first time, I felt like I was part of the Guard Family.

By the time Jon and the rest of his company returned from Cuba in December 2002, we knew war with Iraq was a very strong possibility. In 2003, other Guard friends (including Steve) were called up for duty in Iraq. The country was now fully aware of the fact that the Guard was part of the total Army concept. When the action started in March that year, our Soldiers were in harm's way. The National Guard was front-page news. It was Lynn's turn to juggle single motherhood and a full-time job. The difference was that their daughter was old enough to know that her Daddy was going to be gone for a long time.

It hasn't been easy for military families. Iraq and Afghanistan are extremely dangerous and a typical deployment lasts for one year.

As our troops continue to come and go, it now seems almost normal. We are used to this new reality. September 11 seems a life time ago. We are no longer reacting to an attack; we are executing a long-term strategy to bring security to the Middle East and, in doing so, bring security to ourselves.

It's hard to stay fired up for the long haul. Nobody likes war and when Citizen-Soldiers are killed in the line of duty, it is especially hard on their communities. Most of us know people who have been injured or killed in Iraq or Afghanistan. We want their sacrifice to mean something. Our Soldiers want to complete their mission. They want to <u>win</u>. They want Americans to know that even though we are fighting a complex and determined enemy, good things are happening, too. Sometimes it's hard to keep our eye on the ball. For me, the hardest part is biting my tongue when people say things like, "I support the troops, just not the war." Why is it important to make that clarification? I'd rather have them say, "Thanks for your service!" But that's just me.

With all the emphasis on Iraq and Afghanistan, we sometimes forget that duty doesn't begin and end in the Middle East. While much media attention has focused on the Guard's involvement in the War on Terrorism, family members know that Soldiers are constantly on call for other important missions as well. In September 2005, for example, Americans saw the devastation of Hurricane Katrina. In the midst of the crisis, the family members of 21,000 National Guard troops packed up their Soldiers and sent them away on a few days notice. Jon was the company commander for the 178th Military Police Company in Monroe, Georgia, (Hooah!) and the day after Katrina, I cancelled our long-planned and highly-anticipated trip to attend the National Guard Association of the United States (NGAUS) conference in Hawaii. The morning he left, neither of us knew where on the Gulf Coast he would be working, his specific mission, or when he would be home. Neighbors, some of whom I had never met, dropped off dozens of bags full of supplies such as baby wipes, hand sanitizer, foot powder, and bottled water for the men and women in Jon's company.

My personal contribution was a case of Alpo and a can opener. I knew the Army would take care of the Soldiers. But who would take care of the dogs? As it turned out, one of the Military Police Officers in Jon's company was a veterinary assistant in her civilian life and set up an animal triage unit on a tennis court. She used her connections to get personnel and resources to help the Katrina animals. Only a National Guardsman could offer such a skill set!

The Gulf Coast effort was the Guard's largest natural disaster support operation ever. In fact, it was the largest military disaster response mission ever. The experience taught me how important National Guard Soldiers are to the communities that they live and work in. They provide their families, friends, neighbors, and co-workers one degree of separation from important events. My neighbors felt helpless and wanted to do something right away. Having a Citizen-Soldier in their circle allowed them to do so immediately.

And it never ends. In 2006, President Bush ordered 6,000 Guard members to help secure the Mexican border. At the same time, the National Guard is fully involved in the planning and execution of the nation's response to a potential pandemic outbreak, and many other unforeseen events and emergencies will require the rapid response that only the Guard can provide. Isn't it exciting to be so close to the headlines? I think so. The bottom line is there is no such thing as a weekend warrior anymore. And if there is, it is one l-o-n-g weekend!

There is a big difference between the lifestyle of an active duty military family and the family of a Guardsman. We are not professional military spouses and our children are not official Army Brats (brats, perhaps, but not Army Brats, which, I was surprised to find out, is an endearing term used by military families themselves). You and I are regular citizens living in regular communities spread across the landscape. We don't live on-post. We don't shop at the Post Exchange (PX). We don't have a built-in support structure of other military families close at hand. We do our best to support our Soldiers while we balance our own careers and families. Our Soldiers have full-time careers that they must manage. It is challenging in a best-case scenario, but when our Soldiers are deployed, our lives are affected in a way that is distinct to the Citizen-Soldier.

For ten years, I've tried to find a book for National Guard family members. In my search, I've come across some excellent military lifestyle titles, but there wasn't a single book just for us, until now.

Before you start reading, I would like to clarify something: I'm neither a military expert nor a model military wife. I don't know everything there is to know about the National Guard but I am an eager student and learn something new every day. My intent is to provide a regular person's view of the National Guard world. I focused on areas that I think require a closer look. Rather than recycle information that you can find online, I tried to provide new insight in the areas that are most relevant to Guard family members. My viewpoint will be influenced by my own experience as the wife of an Army National Guardsman.

I know the information in this book will be useful to spouses of those who serve in other reserve forces (Air National Guard, Army Reserves, Naval Reserves, Coast Guard Reserves, Marine Corps Reserves, Air Force Reserves, and State Defense Forces), but the primary audience is Army National Guard spouses. One more thing: I'm not in the Army and wouldn't last a day in it! If your Soldier peruses this book, s/he may chuckle at my oversimplification in some areas. That's fine because this book is for you. That's all a big fancy disclaimer that means consider this more of an essay than a research paper.

I've come a long way from the Madison Avenue working girl lucky just to keep a few acronyms straight. First and foremost, I am proud to call myself a military wife. Being a member of the Guard community is inspiring. I have met so many wonderful people over the years and they are all great Americans. Honor isn't exactly a commodity these days, but it's good to know it still exists. One need not fly to Hollywood or attend a sporting event to see a real hero. Real heroes live among us. They are the men and women of the National Guard. And because you help them do their job, you are elevated to idol status, too.

People always say to Guard family members, "I don't know how you do it." Well, I'm not sure how we do it either, but we do. We just do. Thank you for doing your part. I hope this book will help you in your journey. God bless you. God bless your Soldier, and God bless the United States of America!

I've never agreed that "it takes a village to raise a child," but I am convinced it "takes a village to write a book." Here are some of the people in my Guard "village" who contributed their time, advice, and talent to this project:

Theodore P. "Ted" Savas, Sarah Keeney, Kim Rouse, Veronica Kane, Helene Dodier, Lee Merideth, Lindy Gervin, and the entire team at Savas Beatie publishing. Ted is a true patriot who understands the unique lifestyle of Citizen Soldiers and their families. If you ever need a great promotion or retirement gift for a Guardsman, check out Savas Beatie's extensive catalog of military history titles and reference books at www.SavasBeatie.com or in your local bookstore.

The following members of the Georgia Army National Guard: MG Lawrence H. Ross, Sr., Col. Gregory B. Edwards (Retired), Col. Timothy Romine, LTC Jeff Soracco, MAJ Jeff Daigle, MAJ Ed Laster, MAJ John Lowe, MAJ Anthony Poole, CPT George Arp, CPT John M. Fuchko, III, SFC Christopher Logue, and Mrs. Altamese H. Finch—you may not remember helping me, but you did—thanks!

My fellow National Guard wives: Andrea Laster, Lynn Draper, Star Henderson, Meredith Adams, Doreen Worden, and all of the dedicated Georgia FRG Leaders and members who filled out surveys and shared their perspective.

Thanks also to Ms. Renee Hylton—longtime historian at the National Guard Bureau who reviewed and edited this entire manuscript. I hope you are enjoying your retirement! And to Renee's replacement, Mr. Bill Boehm, who has provided invaluable input and support.

My sisters Anne Forbes and Sheila Kihne. Thanks for asking "how is the book going?" Without your advice and support, I would still be staring at a blank screen.

Finally, I would like to thank my husband, Jon Roscoe, for bringing me into the Guard Family.

Chapter 1

A Brief
History Lesson

*"Every citizen who enjoys the protection of a free government owes not only a
portion of his property but even his personal services to the defense of it."*

— George Washington

Welcome to the Family. Congratulations! You are a member of an
upstanding family with a long and honorable tradition. As I have come to
understand since marrying a Guardsman, your Soldier isn't involved in
some weird, paramilitary version of the Elks Club. He or she is a member of
our Department of Defense, with constitutional powers and responsibilities.

Okay, but it's not really the Army, is it? Well, yes, it is part of the Army
—the oldest part. In fact, it's older than the United States by more than a
century. That's because the National Guard traces its roots back to the
militias of the 13 original U.S. colonies. Its oldest units, which are all in
Massachusetts, can trace their history in an unbroken line back to 1636—just
16 years after the Pilgrims landed at Plymouth Rock.

The opening shots of the American Revolution were fired at Lexington
and Concord in 1775 by local militia and by Minutemen who were recruited
from the militia, and that's why the Minuteman is still the Guard's unofficial
symbol. When George Washington took command of the Continental Army
in 1775, it was a collection of militia regiments. Washington himself began
his military career in the Virginia militia. Since then, 19 other presidents
have been Guardsmen, right up to George W. Bush, who served in the Air
National Guard (ANG).

Before there was an Army or Navy (both founded in 1775) or, for that matter, a United States of America, there was a citizen militia. On December 13, 1636, the North, South, and East Regiments were formed in the colony of Massachusetts. The notion of part-time soldiering is a result of America's earliest English colonies having to be responsible for their own defense. English military tradition depended on the organization of all able-bodied male citizens into militias. This tradition was brought to the new land.

Originally, these militias defended their families and communities against foreign invaders and Indian attacks. Eventually, the Continental Congress put out a call to the colonial militias to fight the Revolutionary War. What we consider today as our Active Army (aka: "Regular Army" or "Standing Army") was actually born out of colonial militias.

After we gained our independence, the Constitution empowered Congress to "provide for organizing, arming, and disciplining the militia and for governing such part of them as may be employed in the service of the United States." Since the colonists had successfully thrown off the imperial designs of the world's largest military, it's easy to understand why our earliest citizens weren't too gung-ho about jumping into another centralized government. Thus, in the same clause, our Founding Fathers wisely left the training of Soldiers and appointment of officers to the commands of the individual states. Today's National Guard follows the same model.

The name National Guard came into being in 1825 when the 2nd Battalion, 11th New York Artillery, acting as honor guard for the Marquis de Lafayette during his visit to the United States, used the name in recognition of his service as commander of France's "Garde Nationale" during the French Revolution. During the balance of the 19th century, New York and many other states adopted the term National Guard for their militia. It was mandated by Congress that all state militias be designated as National Guard in 1916.

The Oldest Units In The Army

Four Massachusetts Army National Guard units trace their lineage to the 1636 organization of militia regiments in the state. They are the 101st Engineer Battalion, 101st Field Artillery Battalion, 181st Infantry, and the 182nd Cavalry. All four share the distinction of being the oldest units in today's Total Army.

Act One: The First Transformation

Throughout the nineteenth century, our young nation held

fast to its revolutionary ideals. Unlike European nations with large, standing armies, our country kept a small—I'm talking 10,000 small—active-duty army that relied on the militia units and wartime volunteers to provide the bulk of troops when necessary. The pattern established in the early part of the nineteenth century remained in place through the War of 1812, the Mexican War (1847), the Civil War (1861), and the Spanish-American War (1898).

But this system would not last much longer. As the century drew to a close, Americans became increasingly concerned about a large nation relying on such an ad-hoc method of national defense. In particular, the Spanish-American War brought weaknesses to light that could bring disaster in any future conflict with the world's great imperial powers.

The National Guard as we know it today began to emerge in the first years of the 20th century. The Militia Act of 1903 began a process that has continued for more than 100 years: the federal government provided increased funding and equipment for the states' National Guards, and in exchange, the National Guard had to meet federal standards in order to get that increased funding. The Congress spent the next several years proposing plans for a twentieth-century army, and in the landmark Militia Act of 1903, the roots of the National Guard that we know today came to be.

Official US Military Alphabet

Have you ever been asked to spell your name out over the phone? It can be confusing. The person on the other end thinks you said "D" when you said "B" or "Y" when you said "I." Military members use a Phonetic Alphabet to spell letters in place of just saying the letter itself. By saying an entire word versus a single letter, there is less chance that the person listening will confuse letters. In addition to military use, the phonetic alphabet is used in radio communications around the world by ships, aircraft, and amateur radio operators.

A: Alpha	N: November
B: Bravo	O: Oscar
C: Charlie	P: Papa
D: Delta	Q: Quebec
E: Echo	R: Romeo
F: Foxtrot	S: Sierra
G: Golf	T: Tango
H: Hotel	U: Uniform
I: India	V: Victor
J: Juliet	W: Whiskey
K: Kilo	X: X-Ray
L: Lima	Y: Yankee
M: Mike	Z: Zulu

This legislation—also known as the Dick Act (because it was sponsored by Senator Charles Dick, a major general in the Ohio National Guard)—increased funding and granted Federal status to the militia. This meant that state militias needed to conform to Regular Army standards from this point forward. To do this, new provisions were made including:

- National Guard units would attend twenty-four drills and five days of annual training a year.
- National Guard Soldiers would be paid for annual training.
- Militia units were subject to inspection by Regular Army officers.
- All enlisted Guardsmen were issued complete uniforms and equipment to match that used by the regular Army.

Within five years, the desire of the Army for a wholly federal version of the Guard began to be slowly realized.

Act Two: The Militia Becomes the National Guard

In 1916 legislation was passed that required all federally-funded units and Officers to be federally recognized in order to get federal money. But in return, Guardsmen would be paid for their drills, or training sessions, in addition to the encampments for which they were already being paid (we'll hear more about drills and camps—and pay—later).

The National Defense Act of 1916 transformed the militia from individual state forces into the primary ground force reserve of the United States. Guardsmen were still under the control of their respective governors, but were now required to take an additional oath to serve the Constitution of the United States and its elected leadership. The term "National Guard" became mandatory. The act also determined that:

- All units would be federally-recognized.
- Officer qualifications would be determined by the War Department.
- Yearly drills would increase from 24 to 48, (a two-day monthly drill) and Soldiers would be paid for drills.
- Annual training days would increase from 5 to 15.

Another important part of this legislation was turning the Division of Militia Affairs into a more autonomous and authoritative body called the

Militia Bureau (which would be designated as the National Guard Bureau in 1933). Whereas the Division of Militia Affairs was headed by a regular Army general appointed by the chief of the general staff, the Militia Bureau's chief would be a Guardsman appointed by the president. The National Guard would now be headed by one of its own officers and be responsible for its own performance.

This legislation also created three new reserve elements: the Officers' Reserve Corps (nearly one third of these Soldiers were medical doctors), the Enlisted Reserve Corps, and the Reserve Officers' Training Corps (ROTC). These organizations were entirely separate from the National Guard and were under the control of the Regular Army, not the separate states.

The final piece of legislation that set the Guard on its current path came in the run-up to the Second World War. The National Guard Mobilization Act of 1933 settled the issue of the National Guard and its use as a reserve component in wartime. The legislation made it a component of the United States Army, regardless of circumstance. Interestingly, it also specified the number designation of the units that we recognize today. The standardized numbering system that the federal government created for the naming of National Guard units within the framework of the complete National Army designated the numbers 1—99 for Regular Army regiments and 100—299 for National Guard regiments. In addition, National Guard unit designations would no longer include the names of their given states. Even today, with the Army transforming into a modular and interchangeable set of unit types and numbered designations, the regimental system still holds true for the Infantry. A quick check of your Soldier's Infantry regiment—not brigade or division—will confirm this.

While hundreds of Guard units were called to federal service for the Korean War, and a much smaller number for the Vietnam War, the Guard's main role during the Cold War with the Soviet Union was to be a strategic reserve in case World War III broke out in Europe. But after the military draft ended following the Vietnam War, the Defense Department no longer had a large pool of cheap draftee labor. So instead of a very large active military made possible because the U.S. had a draft, the nation had to rely more on its Reserve components to meet its military responsibilities. This was the beginning of the Total Force Policy, which said that National Guard and Reserve units were going to be trained and equipped to the same standards as their active duty counterparts.

If it Looks Like the Army and Sounds Like the Army: The Army Reserve

One of the most frequent questions that you will be asked is: What is the difference between the National Guard and the Army Reserve?

On April 23, 1908, the Medical Reserve Corps, the official predecessor of the United States Army Reserve (USAR), was created. This was the Army's first Federal Reserve force and was a peacetime pool of trained officers and enlisted men that the Army mobilized as individual replacements for units in the world wars of the twentieth century. With the Armed Forces Reserve Act of 1952, the Officers' Reserve Corps officially became the Army Reserve and was organized into three statuses: Ready Reserve, Standby Reserve, and Retired Reserve. True to its roots, today's USAR provides the big Army with almost 7 in 10 of its medical officers.

While the National Guard is organized as a parallel military organization of the regular Army, the USAR is organized as a complementary military organization to the regular Army. Another way to look at it is that the Army Reserve is the reserve force of the United States Army. The National Guard is the reserve force of the United States of America.

The United States National Guard (USNG) is a dual state-federal force. It exists as the Army National Guard (ARNG) and the Air National Guard (ANG—the reason for the "R" in the Army's Acronym) in all 50 states, three territories (Puerto Rico, Guam, and the Virgin Islands), and the District of Columbia.

The governor, through each state's Adjutant General, commands the National Guard forces. (Guam and the Virgin Islands have Governors, in Puerto Rico; commonwealth officials control the National Guard). Governors can call up members of the National Guard in times of domestic emergencies or need. Examples include, but are not limited to: local and statewide emergencies, natural disasters, or civil unrest. (The exception is the District of Columbia National Guard, the only National Guard organization with no local jurisdiction. Only the President can activate them during civil and natural emergencies.) In addition to having state responsibilities, the National Guard reports to the President. He is the commander in chief of all armed forces and has the right to mobilize the Guard for federal missions. When this happens, both ARNG and ANG members are instantly on federal duty status and answer to the combatant commander of the theater in which they are operating. Ultimately, however, they answer to the president. The USAR, the Regular Army, and all other reserves (the Navy, Marines, Air Force, and Coast Guard each have their own dedicated reserve force) are Federal forces.

A Different Shade of Blue: The Air National Guard

The United States National Guard (USNG) is a dual state-federal force that includes the Army National Guard (ARNG) and the Air National Guard (ANG). In the preface, we learned of the ANG's contribution after the 9/11 attacks.

The ANG was officially established as a separate reserve component on September 18, 1947. Prior to this, however, National Guard aviation began to emerge in the same fits and starts as did military aviation generally. Early Guard aviation was a product of grassroots efforts by Army National Guardsmen. As early as 1908, a group of enthusiasts organized an "aeronautical corps" at the Park Avenue Armory in New York City to learn ballooning. They were members of the 1st Company, Signal Corps, New York National Guard.

While these two parts form the whole, the numbers are significantly different. In terms of Soldiers and Airmen, there are roughly four Soldiers for every one Airmen in uniform. Moreover, as a specialized "Air Warrior" that, as necessary, has their existence built around large and expensive modern aircraft, and the highly-secured technology that supports them, you're just not as likely to drive right past the front gate of one of their 140+ armories. Still, as a National Guard spouse, it is likely that you will meet members of the Air National Guard—especially if you attend state Guard conventions or Family Programs conferences.

As you read through this book, know that from a spouse's perspective, although there are differences between the ARNG and the ANG, they are closer to each other than any other service. The ARNG and the ANG:

- Share the same basic rank structure—although there are a few nuances. The officer rank, both name and image, is exactly the same. It's on the enlisted side of the house that you'll see differences in both name and authorities. Basically a result of the necessarily smaller structure and highly technical nature of most ANG Units.

- Choose areas of specialty and are compensated according to the same military pay scales based on their rank and how many years they have served. They also receive identical cost of living adjustments.
- Have the same benefits and are eligible for similar bonuses.
- Are members of the National Guard Association of the United States and are likely to attend the same annual state conference.
- Follow military protocol and etiquette. The "rules" for attending an Army National Guard function and an Air National Guard function are virtually identical. In fact, it's likely your state functions will be combined.
- May be called to different types of duty in their states, nation, or overseas.
- Follow the same pre-deployment processes and experience the same challenges during long-term deployment. Family members rely on the same support resources—Family Programs Offices, Family Assistance Centers, and Family Readiness Groups.
- Participate in cross-training. Whether your Guardsman is "blue" or "green"—service lingo for 'sky' and 'ground,' they will increasingly work together in what they refer to as the "Joint environment." And yes, even it has a color—"Purple."

The similarities are enough that while a given Soldier or Airmen will initially enlist or be commissioned into their State's Army or Air National Guard, they work interchangeably at the senior planning levels, such as your State's Joint Force Headquarters. During the course of his career, your spouse will likely work with, lead—and may end up working for—an Air National Guard Officer or Non-Commissioned Officer.

The biggest difference, of course, is that the Army National Guard is a part of the US Army while the Air National Guard is a part of the US Air Force. Thus, just as with their

> ### Brigades and Wings
>
> Even the differences are largely the same:
>
> In this book, when you see Army Platoon, think also Air Force Flight
> For Company, Squadron
> For Battalion, Group
> For Brigade, Wing
>
> You'll find the unit's First Sergeant at the Squadron, just as you would expect to find him at your Spouse's Company.

active duty counterparts, they wear the United States Air Force uniform and the standardized military attire worn by Airmen (men and women) of the United States Air Force. The Air National Guard Airmen attend US Air Force training schools, choose ANG specialties, and use an Air Force Specialty Code, AFSC, while the Army uses Military Occupational Specialty, MOS. A Career in the ANG is organized around the following categories:

COMMAND AND CONTROL		
Air Support Operations	Command & Control	Tactical Air Control Party
Flying		
A-10 Thunderbolt		
Intelligence, Surveillance, & Reconnaissance		
Predator	Reaper	Surveillance
Non-flying		
Band	Civil Engineering	Combat Communications
Engineering Installation	Fire Fighting	Rescue
Security Forces		
Space		
Space		
Special Operations		
Combat Control		
We will learn about the Army National Guard's three main functional areas in Chapter 3.		

When ANG members deploy overseas, they support or work for other US Air Force, Air Force Reserve, and Air Force National Guard units.

Your ARNG Soldier will know Airmen. In most states, the Air National Guard is a very active and embedded part of their state's military department or Department of Defense. In today's vernacular, the State headquarters of your state's National Guard is called the Joint Force Headquarters. This is the central point of contact when the Governor needs military units for an event or mission.

Act Three: Weekend Warriors

The State Defense Force

Few Americans are aware of the existence of State Defense Forces. State Defense Forces are a non-paid, all-voluntary militia whose primary function is to assist the National Guard with local or statewide emergencies or provide support to Guard members and their families. Unlike the National Guard, state defense forces serve only at the order of state governors and cannot be activated for federal duties and most groups do not train with weapons.

If you bump into a member of the State Defense Force, you will think they are a Guardsman. They are given military titles but usually have to buy their uniforms, which differ only slightly from active federal and National Guard uniforms.

Twenty-one states now have State Defense Forces, while almost every other state is considering their creation. States with State Defense Forces include Alabama, Alaska, California, Indiana, Louisiana, Georgia, Maryland, Massachusetts, Mississippi, Montana, New Mexico, New York, Ohio, Oregon, South Carolina, Tennessee, Texas, Utah, Vermont, Virginia, and Washington.

So how did all of this activity result in what we recognize as the "one weekend a month, two weeks in the summer" National Guard? In 1955, legislation passed that required Guardsmen to complete basic training on active duty army installations. This ended the era of citizens being turned into Soldiers at armories. The armories sprinkled across our cities and small towns would be used for weekend drills and to house equipment for individual units (as they still are today), but Soldiers received key training and certifications in the same manner as full-time, active duty Soldiers. National Guard and active duty Soldiers train together at basic training, attend the same leadership schools, wear the same uniforms, and adhere to the same military traditions. It's all for good reason. They train for the same eventuality: wartime service.

Once training was centralized, the chief of the National Guard Bureau focused on securing larger blocks of time to train units. We are so used to having our Soldiers gone one weekend a month that it's hard to believe that Guard

Telling Time, Military Style

Military time is a specific method of expressing time used by the military, emergency services, and other law enforcement entities.

The main difference between regular and military time is how hours are expressed. While the normal time keeping duplicates the numbers 1-12 by using am and pm designations, military time refuses the potential for error by assigning a unique number to each hour. However, regular and military time express minutes and seconds in exactly the same way. When converting from regular to military time and vice versa, the minutes and seconds do not change.

I still have a hard time instantly converting military hours to civilian hours. The trick is to simply add 12 to each hour after noon. So, 1:00 becomes 13:00, 5:00 becomes 17:00 and so on. The following table provides a summary of the relationship between regular and military time.

Regular Time	Military Time	Regular Time	Military Time
Midnight	0000	Noon	1200
1:00 a.m.	0100	1:00 p.m.	1300
2:00 a.m.	0200	2:00 p.m.	1400
3:00 a.m.	0300	3:00 p.m.	1500
4:00 a.m.	0400	4:00 p.m.	1600
5:00 a.m.	0500	5:00 p.m.	1700
6:00 a.m.	0600	6:00 p.m.	1800
7:00 a.m.	0700	7:00 p.m.	1900
8:00 a.m.	0800	8:00 p.m.	2000
9:00 a.m.	0900	9:00 p.m.	2100
10:00 a.m.	1000	10:00 p.m.	2200
11:00 a.m.	1100	11:00 p.m.	2300

units used to train on week-nights. This slowly changed when the Guard Bureau authorized two paid four-hour assemblies on a single calendar day. They also allocated funds to provide chow during each drill day. As a result, some units began to drill on weekends. In 1966, the National Guard Bureau mandated that all units drill on weekends.

Eventually, all new National Guard Soldiers—whether private or lieutenant—were trained in the exact same way as their active-duty counterparts. There was also a consistent method of selecting and commissioning officers (National Guard officers were, and still are, appointed by their respective governors and take an oath to obey both the governor of their state and uphold the Constitution and the officers appointed over them by the president.) .

As the standardization grew from state to state, regular citizens began to notice the traffic and uniforms descending on their small towns one weekend a month. Citizen Soldiers became a part of the American experience, and the term "weekend warrior" was coined.

Act Four: A Force Like No Other

Perhaps the most important transformation of the American military in the last century was the decision, made during the Nixon administration at the end of the Vietnam War, to move to a volunteer force. No military in the world, of comparable size, operated on a volunteer basis. In the late 1960s, the American public's aversion to the draft prompted President Richard Nixon to establish The President's Commission on an All-Volunteer Armed Force. The Commission concluded that a volunteer force was viable and had the potential to be more effective than the current model. Congress allowed the authority for the draft to lapse, and the All-Volunteer Force was born on July 1, 1973.

To abolish the draft while ensuring the United States could meet its defense requirements at home and abroad, the new all-volunteer force required substantial Reserve Components. The Total Force Policy was created to treat the three components of the US Army—the Regular Army, the Army National Guard, and the Army Reserve—as a single force. The Total Force Policy would provide sufficient troops for the nation's security needs without the significant cost of maintaining a large standing-army. It would also create a strong bond between the military and civil society.

After Vietnam, the All Volunteer Force was involved in a series of small operations in Lebanon, Haiti, Grenada, and Panama. While the Army fought a series of hot (armed, open conflict) and cold (no direct fighting) wars around the globe, our National Guard remained almost singularly focused on the Soviet threat. It wasn't until the successful conclusion of the Cold War in the late 1980s that a new model of Guard participation in American military tradition would begin to emerge. Although it has had many names, this is what we refer today as transformation. While transformation seems complicated, it to is really about shaping our military into an organization that can best respond to known and anticipated threats. To do this, we began shifting from large, heavy, over-lapping, and overwhelming forces to smaller, lighter, and more mobile forces that made up for their loss of size with high-technology lethality. The originators of the Total Force Policy intended that if the US military had to fight a war, the Reserve components would be an integral part of the fight. This is exactly what happened in 1990-1991, when we sent forces to Saudi Arabia after Saddam Hussein invaded Kuwait.

This was the first wartime test for our single, integrated, all-volunteer force. More than 62,000 Soldiers from over 200 Army National Guard units were mobilized for Operations Desert Shield and Storm. Guard and Reserve leaders, along with their allies in the Congress and the Department of Defense, spent the remainder of the decade building the Army of One that has performed so magnificently around the world in the current theaters (places of combat) of the Global War on Terrorism (GWOT). While Desert Storm first tested the strength of the total Army, it is the GWOT that has proven the strength of the system because the National Guard has been called to serve in numbers unprecedented since the Second World War. To stabilize Iraq, the Pentagon relied heavily on the Army National Guard. In 2004, for the first time since the early days of World War II some 60 years before, a majority of the actual combat units with boots on the ground in Iraq were Guard units.

In 2008, some of the most significant National Guard reforms since the Dick Act were established. The Authorization Act elevates the Guard's stature in the Pentagon by increasing the NGB chief to a four-star general and making the position a principal advisor to the defense secretary. In addition, a Guard officer will be assigned as the deputy commanding general of the US Northern Command. The Guard Bureau is no longer a joint bureau within the departments of the Army and Air Force, but a joint activity in the

Department of Defense. All of these reforms give Guard leadership a permanent say in Pentagon decision-making. These reforms will help the National Guard meet its current mission to:

- Provide security and defense to our homeland both here and abroad
- Support the Global War on Terrorism—here and abroad
- Provide America with a relevant, reliable, and ready force that is transformed for the 21st Century

Which Brings Us To Today . . .

In today's Guard, deploying to a combat zone for nine months or a year has become routine. It's a long way from the Guard of the mid-1950s when a Soldier could expect to go to drill every month, camp for two weeks in the summer, or be called up by the governor if a flood, tornado, or big snowstorm hit and that was about it. Those days are gone.

I wrote this book to help you understand and cope with the new realities of serving in today's National Guard. Your Soldier isn't a weekend warrior anymore. He or she is a Soldier, who can expect during his or her years in the Guard to be sent all over the United States and all over the world. Our Soldiers are involved in a serious and dangerous profession. They are often in harm's way. Some are injured in the line of duty. Some pay the ultimate sacrifice when they lay down their lives for our country. It is a heavy load to carry. But we carry it because we know that what they are doing is important. We know that our country depends on their duty—and our sacrifice—to be Number One.

In recent years, Americans have been reminded yet again that being in the National Guard is serious business. Our fellow citizens watch the news and see the sacrifices that Soldiers and their families make. Some people feel sorry for us. Others use stories of misfortune to push their own political agendas. Most just want our Soldiers to be safe and sound. And, of course, we do too. But that is out of our control. That is one of the hardest parts of loving a Soldier. Sometimes you feel like you are holding your breath. You ask yourself if it is really worth it. You think to yourself, "Well, if he or she wants to be patriotic, why not just run for city council or something?" But it's so much bigger than that. It goes way beyond patriotism.

One of the most amazing things, to me, is that for all that our Soldiers' sacrifice, you rarely hear them complain. In fact, their enthusiasm is contagious. No matter what the mission is, they welcome it. You get the feeling that they are ready, willing, and excited to put their training and experience to the test. That's when you realize that they love what they do. It is a part of who they are. It's part of the DNA of their character. Being in the Guard makes them who they are. If they weren't a Soldier, they wouldn't be themselves. Our Soldiers are brave, courageous, and patriotic. No matter how big their mission is, you can expect them to do their duty with professionalism and enthusiasm. They have made a choice to serve and by supporting this choice, you are serving our country as well. They couldn't serve without our unconditional support. The family members, friends, and employers of Guardsmen play a vital role in the overall military

HOOAH?

So what, exactly, does "Hooah" mean, and where, exactly, did it originate? Well, the funny thing is that nobody actually knows the answer to either of these questions. There are so many conflicting theories about the origination of Hooah that we aren't even going to get into it. But, in general terms, it can mean:

- Good copy
- Roger
- Good or great
- Glad to meet you
- Welcome
- Yes
- Thank you
- You have taken the correct action
- Amen

Former Army Chief of Staff General Gordon R. Sullivan explains: "It means: we have broken the mold. We are battle focused . . . look at me, I'm a warrior, I'm ready . . . I serve America every day, all the way."

Basically, Hooah is all good. The best part is that YOU can say Hooah too!

Adapted from Rod Powers, "Origins of Hooah." Accessed August 20, 2010,
http://usmilitary.about.com/od/jointservices/a/hooah.htm

organization. We are not talking about a side job. We are talking about a serious and important commitment that affects every part of your life. And it isn't easy. It isn't easy to take care of the kids while your Soldier is doing his or her duty. It isn't easy when your loved one is in harm's way. It isn't easy when you need to reach your Soldier and can't. It isn't easy when mom or dad can't make it to an event because they have drill. It isn't easy when we spend birthdays and holidays without our Soldier. But every time a neighbor or even a stranger comes up and says "thank you for serving" or a child looks at your Soldier in awe, your batteries are recharged. You know that it is worth it. We are all a part of something much bigger than ourselves. And we are in it together. Hooah!

Wrap Up

- Thank goodness that our earliest settlers quickly recognized the obligation to give of their time and military skills to protect the life and property that they enjoyed. This willingness to serve voluntarily laid the framework for today's citizen Soldiers.
- The National Guard has transitioned from a strategic reserve force into an operational force. We needed the correct organization standing by, at the ready, because when nineteen men carrying box cutters boarded four flights that fateful morning, our nation needed the help of its citizen Soldiers. Since 2001, National Guard Soldiers have worked tirelessly to secure our nation and protect our freedom.
- The family members, friends, and employers of National Guard Soldiers have also made sacrifices for a greater good. Our Soldiers do this as volunteers, and because they do, we do too.

Chapter 2

Duty Calls

What is Duty?

In his final address to the Corps of Cadets at the U.S. Military Academy at West Point, General Douglas MacArthur, just months before he died, famously quoted the school's motto of "Duty, Honor, Country" as the guiding principles that he followed throughout his career. But what, exactly, did he mean?

Honorable conduct and devotion to your country are ideas that are readily understandable, but what is duty? Your Soldier says that he is doing his duty. Your husband's duty assignment, your friend's active duty training in the summer . . . how can one small word possibly fit in all of these situations?

At its root, the word "duty" implies an obligation, though it is interpreted in various ways by people in different circumstances. MacArthur felt obligated to defend the honor of his country; a Soldier felt obligated to serve a higher cause than her own self-interest; your husband was obligated to guard the weapons in the armory from the time he relieved the Soldier guarding them before him, until he, himself, is allowed to leave by his replacement. Duty is much more than one small word; it is the heart of everything your Soldier does. Duty is what makes this part-time job a noble profession. But like all things martial, this high, noble concept needs to be defined, practically for the organization. To this end, the ARNG has defined the levels of obligation, or duty status, that individual Soldiers and entire units are responsible to perform.

Call to Duty

So, how, exactly, are National Guard units called to duty? Not sure? Don't feel alone. It's complicated! As outlined in Chapter One, the Guard has both a federal and state mission. These dual requirements mean that your Guardsman is a member of both the National Guard of his or her state and the National Guard of the United States. Because of their dual status, Guardsmen may be activated in a number of ways both as individuals and as part of a unit. Even the weekend drills that our Guardsmen are so famously known for have an official designation: Inactive Duty Training (IDT). The three main regulations governing the way troops are called to duty outside of their normal drill weekends are State Active duty, Title 32 duty, and Title 10 duty.

Regardless of how they are called to duty, there is one common denominator: <u>you</u> will be one of the first to know. How can this be? Simple. Most of the Soldiers in an ARNG unit are traditional Guardsmen. And by most, I mean that typically only three members of your Soldier's 150-person company are not traditional (or M-Day) Guardsmen; they are the full-time, active duty Guard Soldiers known by the acronym AGR. Active Guard and Reserve (AGR) Soldiers are exactly what the name implies—active duty Soldiers that keep the unit running in between the drills that M-Day (Mobilization Day) Soldiers attend once a month. When the call comes down from the unit's higher headquarters that there has been an event that prompted the governor to activate your Soldier's unit, the three AGR Soldiers begin immediately notifying the M-Day Soldiers to report to the armory. Those full-timers will most likely start by pulling up your home number and passing the message on to whomever answers the phone.

State Active Duty (Local Emergencies)

At the end of the Cold War, most Americans could probably tell you that the National Guard provided protection of life and property and preserved peace, order, and public safety when emergencies got too big for the police or other first responders to handle. These local missions are most commonly accomplished working side-by-side with the first responder agencies of your local city and county—the police, fire, sheriff, and EMTs that keep things together on a daily basis. They include:

- Emergency relief support during natural disasters such as floods, earthquakes, and forest fires
- Search and rescue operations
- Support to civil defense authorities
- Maintenance of vital public services
- Counter-drug operations
- Counter-terrorism operations

In this base level of duty status, the governor calls Guard units (and sometimes individual Guardsmen) into state service during emergencies or to assist in special situations which lend themselves to use of the National Guard due to its training and/or equipment.

Our Soldiers are not the only ones in on the adventure. When it comes to State Active Duty missions, you will be front and center as the action unfolds. When Mother Nature threatens your state, the local media will be on the story. If you are in for a major disaster such as a hurricane or blizzard, national media outlets will provide 24/7 news coverage. As you wait for the hurricane to hit or the snows to start, at that very same time, the full-time Guardsmen (the Soldiers on AGR duty) at your state Guard headquarters are hard at work, making sure that when they get the call from your state's Emergency Management Agency, units are ready to deploy. They alert the right units, with the required equipment and make sure everyone anticipated to be needed is contacted.

Since these types of emergencies tend to be late-breaking, even though you will have an idea that your Soldier may be called up, there isn't a lot of time between when he or she gets the call and when they have to pack up and hit the road. Most units responding to Hurricane Katrina in 2005 had one or two days of lead time. A chemical spill, fire, or storm recovery in your area will see units calling their Soldiers for a formation within hours. You can expect your Soldier to be away for several days usually, at most, a week. Depending on the disaster, Guardsmen may be required for extended periods of duty. National Guard units activated under State Active Duty have access to the federally-funded equipment that is kept in its armories and motor pools. All service is performed in accordance with state law. The state leads the effort and must reimburse the federal government for equipment, supplies, and labor costs. In addition, any equipment damaged during operations is paid for by the state. Did the Guard unit use the HMMWV (pronounced Hum-vee) to rescue stranded hikers? Great! Break the axle driving them back to civilization? Your state will have to pick up the tab for the repair.

I was very surprised to discover that Guardsmen put on State Active Duty are not always protected under the Uniformed Services Employment and Reemployment Rights Act (USERRA), as they are if the specific duty performed meets the statutory definition of full-time National Guard duty. Unless the orders issued for State Active Duty cite one of the enumerated Title 32 sections, the duty may not meet the definition of full-time National Guard duty and may not be covered by USERRA laws. Some states have passed laws that protect their Guard members in this situation but others have not. It is up to the states to create their own laws to make sure Guardsmen are protected in these instances. If your state doesn't provide this protection for its Soldiers, you need to get on the horn with your elected representatives and find out what they are doing to make this happen.

Title 32 Duty (State and National Threats and Disasters)

Title 32 duty covers instances where individual units are activated for a primarily federal purpose. The two main areas under this type of duty are:

- Homeland Defense missions (HLD)—Proactive Military/Security Operations
- Homeland Security missions (HLS)—Reactive Civil Restoration Operations

The term "Homeland Defense mission" refers to an activity undertaken for the military protection of the territory or domestic population of the United States, or of infrastructure or other assets determined by the Secretary of Defense as being critical to national security. The Defense Secretary also has the authority to provide funds to a governor to employ Guard units or members to conduct homeland defense activities. Homeland Security

The Minuteman Symbol

Who is this Colonial farmer who has put down his plow and picked up his musket? He represents the citizen soldiers who fired the first shots of the revolution at Lexington, Massachusetts. The Army National Guard honors the lineage by incorporating the minuteman into its official logo.

missions are those in which the Guard supports the efforts of civil authorities.

As in the case of State Active Duty, the governor is still the commander in chief, but in essence, he or she is answering the president's call for troops. The phrase "the president has declared the region a national disaster area" means that the federal government will foot the bill for Title 32 duty. A great example of Title 32 duty performed for an HLD mission was the airport security mission after 9/11 when so many people across the country became acquainted with uniformed Soldiers as they traveled. What they may not have realized is that almost all of these Soldiers were National Guardsmen. Guardsmen defended their individual states as part of a larger, national homeland defense mission.

The Uniformed Services Employment and Reemployment Rights Act

The Uniformed Services Employment and Reemployment Rights Act (USERRA) prohibits discrimination against persons because of their service in the Armed Forces Reserve, the National Guard, or other uniformed services. USERRA prohibits an employer from denying any benefit of employment on the basis of an individual's membership, application for membership, performance of service, application for service, or obligation for service in the uniformed services. USERRA also protects the right of veterans, Reservists, National Guard members, and certain other members of the uniformed services to reclaim their civilian employment after being absent due to military service or training.

Another example of Title 32 duty was the nation's response to the twin disasters of 2005: Hurricanes Katrina and Rita. This was a Homeland Security mission, performed in federally-funded Title 32 Status because the Soldiers involved operated outside of their state jurisdictions.

Put another way, Title 32 is a war mobilization for a situation inside of the Continental United States (or CONUS, pronounced Coh-nus). In this case, there are no hotel rooms, no evenings off, and no chow at Burger King. Soldiers are deployed domestically. They stay at the site of the incident in tents and are eating MREs (meals ready to eat). They may not know exactly what their duties will be until they get on site. Don't count on any immediate communication from them. You may get a call within a few days of their departure but there won't be a lot of time to chat. Vital information will flow through the unit Family Readiness Group calling tree that is discussed in Chapter Eight.

Title 10 Duty (Overseas Deployment as Armed Forces of the United States)

Title 10 duty covers instances when the National Guard is mobilized for a federal mission. This includes the deployments in support of Operations Iraqi Freedom and Enduring Freedom in Afghanistan. Command and control of all troops rests solely with the president and the Army. As the authority to call up units and/or individuals is written in Title 10 of the U.S. Constitution when this provision is implemented, the result is known as serving in a Title 10 status or federal active duty. Army Officers can now command Guard troops and units which normally does not occur when they are in state status. When a Guard member is on Title 10, he or she is indistinguishable from the other military personnel in the eyes of the government. They are paid the same amount of money (based upon rank), receive the same combat and housing allowance pay, are eligible for the same medical/dental benefits (as are their dependents), and receive the same death benefits as all Army Soldiers. The time spent on Title 10 counts as federal active service exactly the same as active duty Army time. The deployment cycle for this type of service has a much longer lead time. Soldiers will train for their mission at one of the Army's active duty installations for weeks or months before being deployed overseas. The length of deployment is based on the mission performed and is subject to extension.

Obviously, the most recognizable example of Title 10 duty is the mobilization of ARNG divisions, brigades, regiments, battalions, and separate companies in support of the Global War on Terrorism. Since September 11, 2001, virtually every unit of the National Guard, a force the size of the entire active Army, has served on active duty for one or more of the deployments at home or abroad. As noted in Chapter One, the last time that the entire National Guard was mobilized was for World War II. A typical Guard unit should expect to be mobilized about once every five or six years; although some, due to their mission specialties such as Special Forces, may serve more frequently.

How Individuals are Called to Active Duty

Typically, in the case of State Active Duty, Title 32 duty and Title 10 duty, Soldiers are activated with their units. However, Guard members can also be activated as individuals. The three main reasons that Guardsmen are put on active duty individually are:

- Schools or ADT (Active Duty for Training); This includes resident courses such as Airborne, Air Assault, NCO schools, MOSQ (Military Occupational Skill Qualifications) courses, etc.
- Individual Mobilization Augmentee (IMA); As individual subject matter experts for augmenting, deploying or already deployed units.
- Casualty Notification and Assistance Officers; As Commissioned and Noncommissioned Officers assisting surviving family members in the aftermath of the death of a Soldier.

Schools

Soldiers attend military schools during their career for the same reason that other professionals attend college, to gain or update their skills so that they can take part in the higher areas of their career field. Many of these courses are no more than two or three weeks in duration, which—you guessed it—falls in sequence with the traditional two-weeks a year training that is required of Reservists. The lion's share of these mini-activations is for professional advancement or skills refresher coursework. In addition to required training and coursework, there are additional skills-training courses open to qualified Guardsmen. Your Soldier will train with his active Army counterparts to master a specific skill. Do they want to jump out of an airplane, learn a foreign language, or try a different military career field? If your Soldier has the time, there are plenty of opportunities. Not only will it not cost you a dime, your Soldier will get paid for attending the course plus their travel, lodging, and meals are covered. If your Soldier is flying to their course, their ticket will be purchased for them. If they are driving their privately-owned vehicle, they will be reimbursed for the mileage.

Individual Mobilization Augmentee (IMA)

The Individual Mobilization Augmentee volunteers to fill a position in an active Army or Reserve Component unit. In rare cases, those with special qualifications may be assigned to the Selective Service System or the Federal Emergency Management Agency (FEMA). The position requires a specific skill set and is rank and MOS-dependant. The other term bandied about for this type of status is COTTAD (pronounced, Coh-tee-tad) for Contingency Operations Temporary Tour of Active Duty. As the name of the process implies, it sets a hard and fast limit on the amount of time that your Soldier will be away, as well as where and with whom the tour of duty will be performed. Individual mobilization augmentees train on a part-time basis with the appropriate organization to prepare for mobilization and the amount of training is decided by the specific component's policy.

Casualty Notification and Casualty Assistance Officers

This is perhaps the noblest duty that a Soldier can perform—assisting our fallen warriors and their families as a Casualty Notification Officer (CNO) or Casualty Assistance Officer (CAO). In the military, a Soldier becomes a casualty when he or she is reported as injured, ill, missing, or dead. For each instance, the Army has a very specific procedure for notifying the Soldier's family. If the member is injured or ill, the family will probably be notified by telephone. If he or she is killed or missing, the family will always be notified in person by a CNO. After contact is made, a CAO will take over to assist the family members. Their mission is to provide assistance to the primary next-of-kin and/or the person authorized direct disposition of the Soldier's body following his death. In the case of a missing Soldier, the next of kin are advised of what information is available.

CNO and CAO jobs are on the duty roster. Every state keeps a list of Soldiers who are trained for this role and able to perform this duty. For the sake of logistics and readiness, there are many full-time Guardsmen on this list. However, M-Day Guardsmen often volunteer for this duty and can perform CNO duty in lieu of their two-day drill. The CNO is assigned based on geography, not unit association. When a CNO/CAO's name reaches the top of the list, it is their turn to perform this duty and it's not a job they can refuse or put off.

If your Soldier is on the duty roster for CNO duty, they will receive a phone call from headquarters to inform them that they will perform duty. This call can come at any time—and on any day. A Soldier should call their civilian workplace as soon as possible to give them notice that they will need a day or two off from work. Most employers are very understanding and happy to do whatever they can to assist a military family in crisis. The CNO reviews the casualty's records and locates his or her next of kin contact information. If the records are outdated or other complications arise, this can take time. Once contact is made, the CNO stays with the family until he informs the CAO that he has discussed the situation with the family. During the discussion between the two Officers, they will also talk about any special needs or immediate concerns that the family has expressed. The Notification Officer will then hand-off the family to the CAO, who will contact them and schedule an appointment to meet at their earliest possible convenience. At this point, the CNO's primary duty is completed. If the Notification member misses a day or two of his or her civilian job and the time needs to be made up, this can be done over their regularly scheduled drill weekend.

As you have probably guessed, this is a formal duty and is performed in Class A, Army green dress uniform with all the ribbons and insignia properly affixed. A Soldier must be professional and empathetic at the same time. Your Soldier is representing the military and the way they conduct themselves has a lasting effect on how the family views the military. This means that they have to go the extra mile to ensure that the family's needs are addressed. If they don't have the answer, they will find the answer. Although there is a process for performing this type of duty, every family's needs are different and no two cases are alike. If there are children to be picked up from school, employers to coordinate, with or things that need to be done, the CAO will take care of it. The CAO will walk the family through the hundreds of decisions that they have to make during a time of incredible pain. They will also help the family complete all of the necessary paperwork. Your Soldier will work with the family from the day of notification until the funeral, financial, and other arrangements are settled and often, well beyond.

This duty takes precedence over all other obligations and responsibilities, military and personal. If the call to duty comes on Christmas Eve, your holiday will be affected. If it comes on your birthday, you will have to celebrate later. Your Soldier will be given the information and instructions necessary for them to commence duty. They will need quiet, uninterrupted time on the phone to get instructions and take notes about the family that they will serve. Give them a hug and let them go. When they return, they will need a soft place to land.

Your heart will go out to the family members who have to deal with such a loss. You will want to do anything and everything you can to help this family. The best thing you can do to help is to support your Soldier and take care of things at home so they can meet the demands that the job requires. If your Soldier is the CAO, the family can call upon him or her day or night. They will have your phone number and if they can't reach him, they will call you. While your Soldier is on CAO duty, you may see some unfamiliar phone numbers on your caller ID. Always pick up the phone and introduce yourself, tell them how sorry you are and help them locate your Soldier.

Being a CAO takes a lot of time. The National Guard understands that this is the number one focus for a Soldier and he or she will be given the flexibility needed to perform this duty. Because of the time commitment required, full-time Soldiers typically perform CAO duty. However, M-Day Soldiers can volunteer and be activated for this assignment.

Active Guard and Reserve (AGR) and Technicians

Along with a civilian staff, full-time Guardsmen augment and support the Guard organization by working at the state headquarters. This is where administrative support functions such as human resources and family programs offices are housed in addition to a small slice of the brigades, battalions, and companies at armories located all over your state. Full-time Soldiers operate within the same rank structure as other Guardsmen and aren't granted any special status within their state organization. They exist to support National Guard units and keep things running smoothly for M-Day Soldiers.

Both AGR Soldiers and Technicians perform day-to-day management, administrative, and maintenance duties. In addition to their full-time duties, both attend monthly drills and AT exercises. The key difference between the two is that AGR Soldiers serve under the command authority of their respective state or territorial governors until mobilized for federal duty. Except in rare cases, they go one place for their day job and their monthly drill. If the unit that they drill with is activated, they will mobilize with that unit. But even AGR Soldiers who work outside of a unit command structure on their weekdays can be activated in connection with the part-time position they hold in a deployable unit on the weekends. AGR Soldiers are subject to the same pay, entitlements, and retirement benefits as their Army counterparts. However, they are not paid for monthly drills or AT; it is considered a part of the profession. Like the state-based version of the active duty Army that they are, if they're needed to perform somewhere else in the state, away they go.

Military Technicians are civil service employees of the federal government who must be military members of the unit that employs them. They are considered dual-status and train, drill, and activate with the unit that they are attached to in their full-time position. Technician pay is based upon government pay tables (versus military pay tables) and their retirement package is the same as that for civilian employees of the federal government. To the outside world however, AGR Soldiers and Technicians appear as the same animal. Both work full-time as part of the Guard organization, both wear a uniform to work every day, and both work together in the same buildings and on the same teams.

For a traditional M-Day Guardsman and their family member, exposure to full-time Guardsmen occurs first at the company level. As I stated at the start of this chapter, within a typical company of 150 Soldiers, there is usually a three-person staff to support the other 147 members: a full-time Staff Sergeant serving as a supply Noncommissioned Officer (NCO), a full-time Staff Sergeant serving as a training NCO, and a full-time administrative Sergeant First Class running the shop in between weekend drills. As the backbone of the unit's management, they tend to be highly visible professionals. Thus, your Soldier will definitely recognize the full-time Soldiers connected to his or her unit.

These staff members are stationed at individual armories and keep the company functioning between drill weekends. If you ever drop by the armory during Monday-Friday business hours, the people who greet you are full-time Guardsmen. If you find yourself at a battalion-sponsored event, you will meet more of these folks. In addition to a few civilian support employees, a battalion headquarters will probably have a Captain (AGR O-3, "O" means officer), serving as a training Officer, a Master Sergeant (AGR E-8, "E" means enlisted) serving as a training NCO, and other AGR staff as necessary to support specific areas and initiatives.

Sounds Great! Where Do I Sign Up?

Soldiers interested in AGR/Technician positions should track openings via their state's online job portal. You will notice that most of the slots available are for E5—E7 pay grades and that very few positions are available for Officers. In addition, as you check further, you will see that every position requires specific experience as well as a specific maximum rank allowable for the job. Position descriptions are very detailed and don't leave a lot of wiggle room. Even though the requirements may seem complicated, your Soldier will know immediately which positions he or she is qualified to apply for and many of my fellow wives are pretty adept at assessing these too!

Guard organizations strive to have a well-rounded talent pool with diverse skill sets and perspectives. Your Soldier will compete against his or her M-Day peers, current AGR/Technicians, Guardsmen from other state organizations, and Soldiers hoping to move from Army service to full-time Guard service. Impressive civilian job experience can set a Soldier apart from his or her competitors. Visibility and connections within the Guard world help too. A Soldier needs to work hard, show initiative, get noticed by their superiors, complete educational and training programs, and do well on their physical training (PT) and test/weapons qualifications. After all of these to-dos are checked off, a Soldier should make their ambitions known to people in their chain of command and seek their mentorship and guidance.

The application requirements for AGR versus Technician are different and outlined in each individual job posting. The process for application varies from state-to-state and from position-to-position. However, each posting will tell the Soldier what is required in his packet and the deadline for submission. It will also dictate any qualifiers. The packet contains similar material to promotion packets, which you will learn more about in *Chapter 5: How Do Promotions Work?* Qualified finalists will be contacted and interviewed in front of a selection board made up of the Soldiers who they would be working with. Interviews are conducted using objective metrics and candidates are scored accordingly.

Something to Consider

While working full-time for the National Guard is an honor and offers many benefits, from a spouse's perspective, it is important to understand that a full-time Soldier will be expected to work long hours. In addition to their full-time and part-time responsibilities, there are additional expectations that must be met without question and sometimes—without much warning. And, rest assured, there is no over-time pay or comp time program offered! As a spouse, you need to be extremely flexible. You should also be ready and willing to become involved with the Guard family on a social and volunteer level. Events that you may have considered optional as the spouse of an M-Day Soldier become mandatory when you are married to a full-time Guardsman.

Perhaps the most important challenge to consider is the complicated logistics of a full-time Guard career. Your Soldier's ultimate career path isn't only determined by his or her performance record, but by the highest level of leadership within your state organization. Every state's Chief of Staff (CoS) is responsible for maintaining a fluid organization that can respond readily to the top-down needs of the Army. In addition, they have to keep both M-Day and full-time Soldiers moving on individual career paths so they can secure promotions.

As a result, full-time Soldiers are often moved to new positions and sometimes into different career fields. If the need arises, a full-time Soldier must be ready and willing to go to any part of the state to perform their duties. You definitely have to be prepared for this type of arrangement and have a family plan in place to accommodate it.

In addition, there are more promotion opportunities available for M-Day Soldiers versus full-time Soldiers and as rank increases, there are fewer full-time positions available. This may require full-time Soldiers to switch from AGR status to Technician status during the course of their career.

Wrap Up

- The Guard has both a state and federal mission. Guardsmen can be called to State Active Duty to help with local emergencies. In this case, he or she will usually have a pretty good idea that they will be called up and the location and general duration of the mission.

- In addition to traditional or M-Day Guardsmen, there are also full-time National Guardsmen. Every company has a few full-timers who keep things running between drills.
- Title 32 duty covers instances where individual units are activated for a primarily federal purpose. The governor is still the commander in chief answering the president's call for troops. Hurricane Katrina is an example of this type of duty as are Homeland Defense and Homeland Security missions.
- Title 10 duty covers instances when the National Guard is activated for a federal mission such as deployments under Operation Iraqi Freedom and Operation Enduring Freedom in Afghanistan. Command and control of all troops rests solely with the president and the Army.
- The Uniformed Services Employment and Reemployment Rights Act (USERRA) prohibits discrimination against persons because of their service in the Armed Forces Reserve, the National Guard, or other uniformed services.
- In addition to being called to active duty with their unit, individual Guardsmen are routinely brought on active duty to attend schools, augment deployed or already deployed units, or serve as a Casualty Notification or Casualty Assistance Officer.
- Both M-Day and full-time Guardsmen can serve as a member of a casualty assistance team. It's an honor to do so, but that doesn't mean it is easy. This is very difficult and requires a delicate balance of professionalism and empathy. Your Soldier will be working on overdrive and you must be there for them; they will need your love and support.

Chapter 3

The Company Line

How it All Fits Together

So . . . where does your Soldier fit into the grand scheme of things? What does he mean when he says "my company is flying to another part of the country for AT." Who is she talking about when she says that "battalion is coming down next month" and why does that mean she's stopping by the armory after work to help out? Help *who*? Why is the Guard unit located in my town deployed overseas, while the Guard unit in my uncle's town is home? These are examples of the types of questions that go through your mind as you learn to decipher Guard-speak.

Lesson One: Different Strokes for Different Folks

When I first joined the Guard family, I didn't know that different Soldiers do different things. I thought that everybody in the National Guard trained to do the same thing. I know it sounds ridiculous, but I was new to military life. I knew that the Guard had both a state and federal obligation and that Jon could be called up at any time to do his duty, but that was as far as my knowledge went.

A few months before we moved to Georgia, I began to suspect that different units served different purposes. Jon told me that he was considering changing his branch. For the past ten years, he served in an infantry unit and now a cross-country move presented the perfect opportunity to reassess his career options. He explained that every state has its own mix of units and he wanted to find out the lay of the land in the Georgia Guard. He wanted to check out a cavalry unit (yes, there are still cavalry troops, although we are talking about reconnaissance units driving HMMWVs, not horses) and also considered joining an armor unit. After talking to a personnel Officer at State Headquarters, he signed on to a Military Police (MP) company. I didn't know what, exactly, that meant or why he made this decision. I was pleasantly surprised how easy it was to make a change and transfer to a different states' Guard. As far as his new branch was concerned, he explained all of the details to me, but it went in one ear and out the other. Like I said, it didn't affect me. He would still be gone one weekend a month and two weeks in the summer.

Life was Much Simpler Back in Those Days, Right?

After 9/11, I became very interested in how Guard units were organized. In the short weeks leading up to our mission in Afghanistan, I found it interesting that all of the retired Generals providing military commentary on the 24/7 news networks could effortlessly predict the types of units that would be activated for the expected mission. I wondered how Jon knew that MPs would be in high demand when our forces cleared the Taliban out of Afghanistan. I wanted to know more and started asking a lot of questions. To my surprise, the answers were not as complicated as I anticipated.

What Does My Soldier Do?

If you are a person who (like me) spends an hour looking for your sunglasses only to realize that they are on top of your head, memorizing every different Military Occupational Specialty in the Army is an impossible task. When my husband and I attend his annual Officer's conference, I have a very hard time making sense out of all of the different patches, ribbons, and colors that each Soldier wears. If you really want to know the nitty-gritty details about every branch in the military, I would highly recommend going to the Army's civilian-friendly recruiting website www.goarmy.com; it's all there. Or, you can simply ask your Soldier. For some reason, they have a photographic memory when it comes to insignia. For now, I'm going to keep things as simple as possible.

There are three main functional areas in the US Army: combat, combat support, and combat service support. There are dozens of jobs embedded within each of these areas. Those jobs are called a Military Occupational Specialty (MOS). Every company (or unit) is organized by the type of job Soldiers do. Officers are assigned to a specific branch, while enlisted Soldiers have an occupational specialty. Officers also have an MOS, but enlisted Soldiers are most often identified by their MOS versus their branch. These designations tell us what each Soldier does in the Guard. Whether an Officer branch or an enlisted specialty, the biggest difference between Soldiers is what they train to do at their armories. The table below is a "cheat sheet" that I created to help me get my arms around the big picture.

Functional Areas	Purpose	A Great Place for a Soldier who Likes to…
Combat • Infantry (rifles) • Artillery (cannons) • Armor (tanks) • Aviation (helicopters) • Air Defense Artillery (missiles) • Combat Engineers (bridge or blow up obstacles) • Special Operations (counter-insurgency)	• Engage with and destroy the enemy.	…get dirty and be adventurous.
Combat Support • Chemical (Bio-defense) • Military Police (security) Signal (radios) • Military Intelligence (strategy) • Engineer (construction) • Civil Affairs (outreach) • Psychological Ops (counter-insurgency)	• Provide operational support to the combat arms so combat soldiers can do their job non-stop.	…see the big picture of not just "how" the Army does things but "why" the Army does things. …have a military career that jives with their civilian career.

Functional Areas	Purpose	A Great Place for a Soldier who Likes to...
Combat Service Support • Finance (payroll and purchasing) • Adjutant General (personnel) • Quartermaster (supply) • Maintenance (fixing) • Transportation (shipping) • Chaplain (well-being) • Judge Advocate General (legal) • Medical • Medical Service • Dental • Ordinance (bullets and bombs)	• Provide the logistical and administrative support infrastructure required to keep the Army "at the ready."	...challenge themselves by putting their administrative and technical skills to good use in the service of their country, while bringing brick and mortar experience back to their employer.

The MOS is a job classification system that uses a series of letters and numbers to identify different jobs in different fields. Although the MOS doesn't mean much to us, one look at an MOS and your Soldier can tell you what job that person does. As an example, a 77F (refueling specialist) is an enlisted Soldier who could be assigned to an aviation unit, an artillery unit, an armor unit, etc. This Soldier will wear the branch insignia of the unit where they are currently assigned. An Officer, on the other hand—say a 15B Apache Pilot—may wear an Aviation branch insignia throughout their career even if he or she is assigned to an infantry unit as a liaison Officer.

Confused? No worries. You don't need to crack Military Occupational Specialty codes. The big takeaway is that there are many options available to Guardsmen and most of these specialties are a perfect complement to a civilian career. Unlike the Army, Guard members have a lot of long-term flexibility when it comes to their jobs. Though most Soldiers stick with one specialty for the duration of their military career, they are allowed to change their mind. Sometimes, changes in their civilian world jobs influence their military career. Other times it is a reorganization of the number and types of units a state organization maintains that provides a catalyst for change. Drilling at an Engineer battalion in Buffalo, but just had your civilian firm transfer you to Atlanta? No problem. The New York ARNG transfers your Army paperwork to Georgia and the 78th Troop Command finds you a position as an Engineer at an armory thirty minutes from your front door. Spent your college years at the University of Minnesota learning to kick down doors as a member of the 34th Infantry Division on drill weekends, but used your criminal justice degree to land a job with the LAPD? Great! You can ask your unit to contact the California Guard and they will help you secure an MP Officer slot before you even leave school. With enough planning, it is very possible for your Soldier to move to a different state without missing a single drill.

Whether a Soldier leverages his military specialty to further his success in the civilian job market or is a button-down accountant who likes to blow things up on the weekends, the Guard will accommodate them. A Soldier can stick with his specialty for his entire career or change his MOS; either way, they will be able to plug back into the Guard organization without a hiccup. In fact, switching branches is quite commonplace.

Where Does He or She Go Every Month?

The company is the center of gravity. While the Army has companies too, the company is everything in the Guard. It is where the military world connects with the civilian world and where the rubber meets the road. There are more than 3,000 armories across the country and most of these buildings are home to one or more companies. Nearly eight out of every ten Guardsmen will operate within a company structure for most of his or her career. The entire Army is built around the concept of the company and it is, as the Army says, "the lowest level of employment." This means that a company houses the perfect number of people required to accomplish a given task. Is it the largest group of Soldiers organized? No. A company never has more than 200 members. Is it the most powerful? No. There are many things that a company can't accomplish alone. Is it the most flexible? No. That would be a platoon which is generally about one fourth the size of the whole company and is routinely used to accomplish many smaller missions. But, at about 150 people, a company has the perfect amount of personnel to accomplish a mission, keep track of the people assigned to the mission, and fix anything that gets broken on said mission.

Companies are organized according to branch specialty. For example, if the armory in your town is home to an artillery unit (an artillery battery, actually), ninety percent of the Soldiers in that company/battery will have the same MOS. The company commander will be an artilleryman, the lieutenants will be artillerymen, the NCOs will be artillerymen, and the enlisted Soldiers will be artillerymen. They are all trained to do the same job; although, some have more training than others based on their rank and experience (this will be discussed further in *Chapter 4*). Those in the unit who don't share the same branch, but are equally important to the unit's success, specialize in other areas such as cooks, medics, supply, and maintenance personnel. These Soldiers often move from company to company as they are promoted through the system.

Some company support functions are provided by centralized resources located in different armories. If an armor unit needs supplies, they will work with an ordinance unit. If there is a piece of equipment that goes missing, unit leadership requests a replacement that is delivered by a transportation unit. If the unit is hosting a formal event, they will call a Soldier from the Chaplain Corps to say the invocation. This isn't all that different from how private businesses are set up. If you work at an engineering firm, ninety percent of the people will be engineers and ten percent of the people will support the engineers (mailroom, IT, marketing, accounting, etc.). Just remember, even though companies have unique missions, they are managed according to exact standards and all channel into their state Guard organization which, in turn, allows them to seamlessly plug into the Army.

Part-Time and Full-Time Guardsmen

As we touched on in Chapter 2, the vast majority of Guardsmen that you encounter are the traditional M-Day Guardsmen, meaning that they are responsible for weekend drills and two weeks of Annual Training until and unless they are mobilized. They work in their civilian careers and leave home for one weekend a month to report to their armories. Roughly 80-85% of the total force strength of the Guard is made up of M-Day Soldiers, the rest are full-time Guardsmen, essentially active duty Soldiers assigned to your state's National Guard. Full-time Soldiers keep things running before, during, and after drill weekends. In an average company, three or four

Soldiers work full-time. This is the method the Guard relies on to be an incredibly cost-effective military organization. Taxpayers don't want to foot the bill to keep a bunch of Soldiers on full-time active duty. This makes it possible for the military to push the training of Soldiers and maintenance of equipment to the individual states. Federal dollars flow into the states to support this equipment, but it is much more affordable to pay Soldiers once a month and two weeks in the summer than pay for their full-time active duty equivalents. For their part, state governments are only too happy to have as many units as they can field because they provide the kind of man-power and equipment needed during emergencies.

How the Company is Organized

A company includes up to 200 Soldiers (150 is the norm) and is directed by a senior command team consisting of the Commander (CDR), Executive Officer (XO), and First Sergeant (1SG). Each company is a fully-contained force and typically has three to five platoons and a headquarters section made up of the leadership and logistics/support team MOSs.

The company is broken down into platoons made up of around thirty Soldiers. Each platoon is led by a Lieutenant (1LT or 2LT) with assistance from a Sergeant First Class (SFC). Their job is to train Soldiers to function in the unit's primary mission role. Lieutenants typically stay with a unit for two to four years and rotate out when they are promoted to Captain (or, if they are selected, stay on with the company as commander). The SFC is the platoon sergeant, which, like the company commander, is a duty position, not a rank. Most platoon Sergeants rose up through the ranks at the home unit and know who is who and how things work. Every couple of years, a new commander rotates into a unit. The long-serving enlisted senior Noncommissioned Officers ensure unit stability from year-to-year.

Each platoon typically breaks down into three squads, though a few branches have sections rather than squads. Squads include two teams of eight-ten enlisted Soldiers (mainly Specialists and Privates) and are directed by a Staff Sergeant. A squad is the most basic unit in the military and is almost like a family element. Soldiers in a squad do everything together and often form strong bonds with each other.

THE TRAINING YEAR

IDT: The Weekend Drill

Inactive Duty Training or weekend drill, takes place over a Saturday morning and afternoon with the Soldiers released for the evening and is completed Sunday morning and afternoon. However, depending on the kind of weekend training that is planned, a drill can start on a Friday evening and go through to Sunday evening. What determines the length? The Unit Training Assembly (UTA). The UTA is defined as a four-hour period during which military affairs are carried out. Before World War II, Soldiers usually drilled one night a week for four hours. But after World War II, as equipment became more complex, units needed to spend longer amounts of time training, and the weekend drill was born.

Why a UTA? Why not just a day? Because the UTA is the equivalent of a day's training in the Army and four of them (a weekend's worth) will net your Soldier four days of pay. Soldiers refer to this as a MUTA (Multiple Unit Training Assembly, pronounced mew-tah). Is your husband going to be home Friday evening? If it's a MUTA 4, he will be. Will you see your girlfriend at the movies Saturday night? Not if she has a MUTA 5 scheduled.

Never fear, most drill weekends are MUTA 4s, because there is a ridiculous amount of additional overhead in feeding and housing 150 people for an overnight stay at the armory. But if they have a MUTA 5 scheduled, they will stay overnight. Your Soldier will know about the few MUTA 5s held every calendar year well in advance. They must accomplish a lot in a small amount of time and it is a big deal, so try not to complain and don't expect any phone calls.

Most scheduled drills during the course of the year will be MUTA 4s. As the law states, units must perform 48 UTAs in a year.

> **THE BIG Bs**
>
> A *battalion* includes three to five companies (240-800 Soldiers) and a headquarters unit. A battalion is commanded by a Lieutenant Colonel (LTC) and a Command Sergeant Major (CSM) as the senior NCO.
>
> A *brigade* includes two to six battalions (700-4,800 Soldiers) and is commanded by a Colonel (COL) with a CSM as the senior NCO. Guard brigades and battalions spend much of their time planning two major training exercises: Annual Training (AT) and a Field Training Exercise (FTX).

So what do they do with the time? While there's no particular way that a unit needs to conduct an IDT weekend, a few things are standard. The early morning drill opening centers around head-count and flag-raising. After that, the unit disassembles into individual platoons for training. Many Soldiers can spend an entire weekend at their armory and rarely interact with anyone outside of their platoon. The entire company only gathers for the opening, chow, and a final formation. At the close of business, the company once again assembles, accounts for all people and property, retires the colors (takes down the flag for the day), and heads home.

The Commander and First Sergeant try to leave the platoons alone for the first day. This allows squad leaders to teach classes on subjects such as first aid or map reading. Meanwhile, the Officers and senior NCOs will have an opportunity to conduct training meetings and work on future planning. On Sunday, half of the day is devoted to updating Soldier records and perhaps more class work, while the other half is spent cleaning the armory and preparing equipment for a month-long nap. With this accomplished, the company once again retires the colors and heads for home.

APFT: "Let's Get Physical"

If you notice your Soldier really ramping up his or her physical activity and ramping down their calorie consumption, it's safe to assume that a very special drill is fast approaching. This brings us to another unit responsibility: making sure all Soldiers are fit and able to meet the physical demands of their job. The Army Physical Fitness Test (APFT) is a three-event physical performance test used to assess a Soldier's endurance. The intent of the APFT is to provide a baseline assessment regardless of MOS or duty. That's right, every Soldier—from Private to General—must endure an annual APFT. The APFT has three components: sit-ups, push-ups, and a timed run. In addition, Soldiers must meet the weight restrictions set forth in the Army Weight Control Program (AWCP). This isn't a military version of phys-ed. Standards are put in place to ensure all personnel are able to meet the physical demands of their duties under combat conditions and present a fit and healthy military appearance.

Every unit will hold this program once a year and it usually takes place on a Saturday morning. Personnel from within the company, usually the senior NCOs, will act as graders while the rest of the members take their turns performing their test requirements. Some units do the testing at the armory while others head to a local high school track. You would not think two minutes of push-ups, two minutes of sit-ups, and a two-mile run would take this long, but remember, everybody must go through the paces. Performing well on the APFT is an important part of your Soldier's Guard job. The score of this event, including making height and weight goals, are part of your Soldier's promotion points. And the Soldier must pass both the AFPT and AWCP to remain in the Guard. If he fails either or both, time (usually 90 days) is allowed for him to improve enough to pass. Continued failure will mean his dismissal from the Guard.

FTX: "To the Woods"

When the unit has a MUTA 5 drill, the additional hours (usually on a Friday night) are spent covering the unit's move to a major training site to conduct a Field Training Exercise (FTX). The FTX is one of the significant IDT periods in the entire training year and usually involves the culmination of several MUTA 4s worth of training. Field Training Exercises are almost always spread pretty far apart and, for planning purposes, count on two FTXs per year. Generally, the FTXs are scheduled at the same time of year. After eleven years of marriage to a Guardsman, I have a pretty good idea of when to plan family events and can smell a MUTA 5 approaching even if my husband conveniently forgets to mention it. During this long training event, the Guard assesses the training and readiness levels of its units and members of each unit. You can expect a MUTA 5 within a month or two of your Soldier's AT. Live in a state with fierce winters? You will most likely have a Winter AT on a regular basis and should plan on a MUTA 5 in the late fall. Live in a state with Summer AT and you are looking at an April or May long weekend—the non-jargon way that your Soldier will reference a MUTA 5 or, as I prefer to call it, a very long weekend.

Annual Weapons Qualification: "Going to Shoot This Weekend"

A common FTX that you have probably heard of is the annual weapons qualification. This is held on a live-fire range located at one of the Army's forts or National Guard camps in your state. This is one of the few times during the year that every Guardsman shoots actual bullets, or live rounds, at targets. We're talking pistols, rifles, machine guns, grenade launchers, grenade-launching machineguns . . . you know, the works. Weapons qualification is one of the two for record IDT assemblies (the other being the APFT) that often require a MUTA 5 in many units. The reason for the extra time is that your company or battalion will need to travel to, prepare, and make use of a large piece of real estate in order to accommodate every single member being able to shoot several dozen rounds at targets down 500 meter ranges.

AT: "Camp"

If the company is the engine around which this car is built, Annual Training is the Daytona 500. Why is the two to three week AT such a big deal? The people who I interviewed said, basically, because there is no faking it. This means that although anybody can "suck it up" and deal with any amount of misery, physical discomfort, and instructions dished out during a typical drill weekend, it takes focus and determination to get through two weeks of all Guard, all the time. This is work, but not the kind of work that many of us are accustomed to. There is no shopping online from the comfort of an air conditioned office, chatting with co-workers, or enjoying a leisurely lunch.

From the start of the year (October, for government types), the people in your Soldier's brigade are either planning for or conducting the sub-tasks necessary for the next AT. Their calendar is specifically built backwards from the last day of AT, to the month that they're currently in, so that all parts of the organization are in synch with the events that need to happen to ensure everything runs smoothly. AT is scheduled months in advance and the date rarely slips.

Not every unit has a two-week, middle-of-the-summer AT. Some units have year-round AT which means that rather than the unit as a whole having an AT together, they send teams out to support other unit's ATs i.e., medical, maintenance, and headquarters detachments. Some northern units have a Winter AT (complete with white winter camo "bunny outfits"—I found one in my garage). It all depends on the type of unit your Soldier is assigned to and the kind of environment they are expected to operate in.

So . . . Can I Call or See My Soldier?

Your Soldier will probably have time to call you over a regular drill weekend. And they will call you if they have an opportunity to do so during FTX and AT. If I have a pressing matter, I call my husband. But I don't call him just to chat about silly things. If he does not answer, I know that he is busy and wait for him to call me back. Don't call your Soldier over and over again and get mad if they are unavailable or are short with you on the phone. Remember, they are working! In some locations, cell phone service isn't available. And, no, you can't visit your Soldier during his FTX or AT. Consider these times as your training exercise. Both are good test runs for deployment.

The Company at Work

Okay, now for the fun part. Let us see how all of this pulls together in a real-world scenario:

Massive amounts of rain have drenched your pleasant little valley causing localized flooding. The storm also left ice melting all over town. Chaos ensues. What to do, what to do? Call out the Guard! The mayor picks up the phone. He gets your state's emergency management office. "Our bridge is out and half of my town is without power."

The voice at the other end of the line says, "Roger, Mr. Mayor. Let me get started and call you right back."

Most likely, a pre-assembled list is pulled up on a computer screen with all of the right personnel and equipment for just such a disaster. But what do we know so far? The mayor will want security, so an MP company will be sent. Which ones? Well, because the bridge is down, they will send two from opposite sides of the river. It might be nice to have a unit that can set up a portable bridge, so an engineer company is sent. The governor is going to want to be able to communicate with his officials on the scene, so a communication company (a.k.a. signals) will be activated. And, of course aviation and transportation companies will report to the scene to move supplies back and forth. Maintenance companies will move to the perimeter of the disaster to help support the activated units and manpower-intensive infantry companies will be brought on the scene for sand-bagging, clearing of debris, and running search and rescue missions.

Of course, different problems will often require different types of units. The bottom line is the Guard is prepared to render whatever aid is immediately needed to stabilize the situation until civilian agencies can take over the long-term rehabilitation of the area. The Guard may set up a temporary bridge, but it will not stay around to construct the permanent replacement.

After every mission is completed, whether an internal training exercise, responding to a real-time emergency, or finishing a long-planned-for security mission such as when VIPs visit your state, an After Action Review is completed and lessons learned are documented and distributed. Every state Guard knows exactly which types of units to pull for every possible scenario. That is why the retired Generals can tell which types of units will go where. And not only do Generals know this, most Soldiers do too. Different units, different missions, different specialties. All a part of the same organization. Whether a company is activated alone for a stand-alone mission or as part of a larger team, the National Guard has mastered the concept of plug and play. But it always starts with the company, the heart of the Guard.

Wrap Up

- There are three branches in the US Army: combat, combat support, and combat support services. There are dozens of jobs embedded within each branch. Those jobs are called a MOS.
- The company is everything in the Guard. There are 3,200 armories in the United States and all are the home to at least one or more company.
- Most everything that your Soldier will do in the course of a year is built around the FTX and AT. Mark your calendar and use these long weekends to test your readiness for deployment.
- No matter what your Soldier's job is, he or she plugs into a much bigger system. Units are trained to stand-alone or work with other units to accomplish missions.

Chapter 4

Understanding Rank and the Wear of the Uniform

Rank: The Big Picture

If you have been in the National Guard family for many years, you already know the ropes and the players. You understand how rank works. If you are relatively new to Guard life, rank can be confusing. Don't worry about it. You aren't expected to identify medals and patches from twenty feet away and there won't be a quiz to test your aptitude regarding the three tiers of military personnel. But a firm grasp on how the system works will make you much more confident when you attend Guard events and will help you see how your Soldier fits into the big picture.

The rank system is consistent in the Army. It does not matter if you are a full-time Soldier or a Guardsman; it all works in the same way. Certainly, the little things like who knows who and who lives where are of utmost importance for our fellow military spouses married to regular army Soldiers. I have never lived on a military post and don't know how those things work. My guess is that due to their total submergence in military culture and the fact that the military is their spouse's one and only career, rank influences a spouse's day-to-day life much more than for a guard spouse. The quality of housing improves with rank. The people they associate with may be rank-dependant and so on. Since active duty families move frequently, the rank system gives them a way to get acclimated to a new society quickly.

Fortunately, from a spouse's perspective, when it comes to rank, things are a bit more relaxed in the Guard. We bring civilian sensibilities to the table and you will most likely see the same friendly faces throughout the duration of your Soldier's Guard career. Unlike our active duty counterparts, we aren't constantly being reassigned around the world. While it is always important to respect a person's rank, spouses are encouraged to mix and mingle with other spouses, regardless of their Soldier's rank. This makes sense. Most of our friendships and connections reside in the civilian communities where we live and work. On the special occasions where we see our Guard friends, we make the most of it. In addition, our permanent "duty station" allows us the opportunity to form long-term relationships with other Guard families. And if you happen to live in a community with an armory, you see that local relationships are formed by people of all ranks. The bottom line is that your spouse's rank should not affect how you feel about your place in the Guard family.

Why Do Soldiers Need Rank?

Since rank does not exist as a caste system for Soldiers and their family members, why, exactly, do we need it? Rank is the framework the military uses to synchronize hundreds of thousands of moving parts. Both the Army and the National Guard have long-term strategic plans to meet defined end-point objectives or what civilians often refer to as business goals. In both the civilian business world and the military, meeting and exceeding objectives/goals requires active and enthusiastic participation at every level. It also requires clearly-defined roles and responsibilities. When everybody knows what his or her specific job is within the overall organization, the job gets done faster and the quality is higher. When people are confused about what their specific job is (or think THEIR job is telling you how to do YOUR job), things get confusing.

At the unit level, it's easy to see why rank is needed. At any given time, about a third of the Soldiers are actually doing the job, while another third are preparing for, planning, or moving toward the next job, which leaves the final third to clean-up, repair, and report on the work that was just accomplished. In the military, this cycle never ends and requires trained and experienced people to work in harmony to get the job done. While an individual's rank changes, the system never does. Rank serves as a control mechanism that maximizes the duties and responsibilities of individual Soldiers.

Whether your job is raising your children full-time or working for a corporation, your daily activities are probably so structured that rank would be a hindrance. Not so in the Army, whether full-or part-time. Unlike the civilian sector, where leadership personnel often use subordinates to buffer themselves from accountability issues, in the military, rank is designed to hold commanding personnel responsible for break-downs within the system. As the saying goes in the military, "The first rule of leadership is that it is always your fault," or in plain terms, the leader takes responsibility for a unit's success or failure.

The military prepares Soldiers for leadership positions by associating their rank and position with the job that they do. The higher the rank, the more accountability a person assumes. Occasionally, we see this on the news. A few Soldiers do something stupid and the people at the top are held responsible. That is just the way the military works, and every Soldier accepts this. Breakdowns in performance are unpredictable. But rank is predictable. This means that issues can be separated and addressed without the whole system breaking down, and every Soldier from Private to General must operate within it. Even when personality conflicts arise, a Soldier understands that while you may have a conflict with the person, you always respect the rank. The entire system balances itself on this basic premise.

As civilians, we all know what a job description is and where our box is on the organizational chart. Beginning with our first job, we all have our own experience working within a very subjective rank structure. When we start a new job, we keep our fingers crossed that the person we report to is competent and sane. We hope that the cream rises to the top. But that isn't always the case. And if you have ever had to work for an incompetent, lazy, or paranoid boss, you know how their actions (or inactions) can negatively affect an entire team.

In the military, a subjective rank structure would not only be frustrating, it would be dangerous. Imagine if a person could become a commander because their brother-in-law got them the gig. That is why the military can't be subjective. The requirements to get ahead are spelled out at every level and Soldiers who share common ranks are expected to know the same things and perform at the same level. If they want to rise up in the ranks, there is a standard checklist that must be completed before they can be considered for promotion. Even if they have put in their time and completed the checklist, they must compete with their peers to rise in the ranks. Rank is especially important in the Guard because a lot must be accomplished in a condensed amount of time.

Why are There Enlisted and Officer Soldiers?

While the rank system does not change, military strategy does. Although the word strategy has been a business buzzword for a decade or two, the military created the concept of strategy. (If you really want to trace it back, read "The Art of War" written by Sun-Tzu in 500 B.C.; your Soldier may own a copy of this book.) Strategy is the big picture and it changes. Whether strategy is implementing comprehensive immigration reform or creating a democracy in the heart of the Middle East, the military relies on strategies to determine priorities and deploy appropriate resources. But strategies are just words and words don't bring us closer to reaching our goals; actions do. Take, for example, the actions of a Texas National Guardsman operating a remote video surveillance system that helped Del Rio border patrol agents seize 287 pounds of cocaine, or the actions of the "Green Mountain Boys" from Vermont's National Guard Mountain Warfare School that helped train the new Afghan Army. It is people, managers, and workers, Officer and enlisted, who make things happen.

To put it in the most simplistic terms, Officers are managers. As management, an Officer isn't expected to know every little detail of how things work. Most are not experts in any one area but have a general understanding of all areas. Officers prioritize and direct the work of others. The highest ranking Officers (Generals from the Joint Chiefs of Staff, directors of the Departments of the Army, Navy, Air Force, Marines, and Coast Guard) are like CEOs of the world's largest, most well-known corporations. They set the overall strategy and work with high-ranking personnel in the Pentagon and National Guard Bureau to implement the strategy.

In the Guard, the governor is the commander in chief of all state forces. He or she works closely with the Adjutant General (AG) of their state to determine how Guard forces will be utilized during a particular timeframe. Each state will have its own method to deliver the goods to the people in Washington, D.C. (make their recruiting goals) while meeting the unique needs of their individual state, whether that be ramping up for hurricane duty or providing security for an international meeting.

An Officer's main job is to lead their team to pull through and produce results. Generally most people think of Officers as leaders in combat, commanding troops in the field. These are usually the Combat Arms Officers serving in the infantry, armor, and cavalry units. But they also manage multiple initiatives simultaneously while keeping an eye on the big picture. In theater, the Officer is the one who ensures that the supply parts that will be needed a month out are ordered. The Officer is the one who makes sure that the Technicians needed to repair radios will be available when they need to be. The Officer is the one making sure that there are interpreters in training to replace the ones who will soon return to their families. The Officer isn't the one actually doing these things, but the one who makes sure that they are getting done.

Great Officers accomplish pull through by giving their subordinates just enough freedom to get their work done. They manage, but they don't micromanage. If mistakes are made, they correct them as soon as possible or take accountability if they are too late. When the mission is complete, they give credit to the team and understand that their personal advancement is tied to the results that their people produce.

An enlisted Soldier's main job is to implement his part in pull through as quickly and effectively as possible. They are the people who actually get the work done. Some, such as those in the infantry, are the shooters, the Soldiers engaged in direct operations. But most actually keep the infantryman supported so he can continue to do his job. The enlisted Soldier is the person who fixes the tank and runs the wire from the satellite terminal to the tent. He is the person who orders the food, medical supplies, and bullets necessary to carry on the battle. He or she has the technical knowledge to get the job done, whatever the job may be. Enlisted Soldiers are focused on measurable tasks. They are specialists in their particular MOS and provide the manpower necessary to get things done. Great enlisted Soldiers know exactly what is expected of them and never make excuses. They know that their team is only as strong as its weakest link. They listen and they execute. They are organized, efficient, and energetic.

Officers create plans that roll up to support big picture goals. Enlisted Soldiers execute the plan. In civilian terms, marketing creates the plan; the sales force executes it. They provide completely different functions; each job is equally important and one can't succeed without the other.

Enlisted Personnel: How Do You Become Enlisted?

After holding up his or her right hand and taking an oath to serve, a civilian becomes a Soldier. Until 1955, the Guard conducted its own basic training, but since that time all new recruits are sent to Basic Training, a nine-week long training course where Guard Privates train side-by-side with active duty and Reserve Privates at one of the Army's Basic Training centers throughout the United States. Which Basic Training center your Soldier will report to is usually determined by MOS or slot availability. At Basic Training, a Private learns the rules, regulations, and processes of the United States Army. Training is held in the classroom and on the field. Life-saving, map reading, marksmanship, field-craft, and martial arts are taught to these previous civilians to face physical and mental challenges on their own. But more importantly, they learn the camaraderie of teamwork and trust that will be so vital when they join their company platoon back in the Guard world.

Basic Training—For You Too

Consider your Soldier's Basic Training your Basic Training too. Having your Soldier away, completely 100% focused on Army business, is good practice for future AT and deployments. When your Soldier is at Basic Training, expect minimal contact with him or her. They are very busy and on a strict schedule. Send them off with calling cards but don't wait by the phone or expect to hear from them frequently. While they will have chances to call, it will be sporadic. Don't take it personally because it isn't their fault. They will call you when they get the chance. When they DO call, be brief and supportive. Don't guilt them or complain, they have enough people on their case. Don't expect to have deep, romantic conversations or troubleshoot family issues over the phone. They are working in overdrive and have to focus on Army business.

The first correspondence from boot camp will be a form letter that includes his or her address and tentative graduation information (a packet with more details about graduation will be sent out at a later date with information for family members who wish to attend). This may take a couple of weeks and will be sent to the spouse or parents if he or she is single; significant others don't receive official Army correspondence. Sometimes it takes up to three weeks for this letter to arrive. Once you have their address, write immediately and tell others to write. Positive, supportive letters will keep their morale up. You may want to send them a care package. Before you do this, it is best to ask them what they would like. They may prefer just receiving letters. It goes without saying that you should NEVER send anything goofy that could be an object of ridicule. Don't send a photo of you in your bikini unless you are okay having it posted on a bulletin board somewhere. Save the stuffed teddy bears and glitter for another time. Write your Soldier often. This is the best way to support them while they are away. P.S. During all of your separations, save all your correspondence and ask your Soldier to do the same. You will cherish these letters forever.

Following the end of Basic Training your Soldier will attend an advanced school to learn the skills required to work in their selected MOS. As with Basic Training, these are Army schools and he will be taught by Army instructors and will work beside his counterparts in the Army and Army Reserve. Depending on what MOS the Soldier is qualifying to achieve, these schools can last from a couple of weeks to several months. And not all graduates immediately attend their MOS schools. Because many Guard Soldiers have non-military responsibilities such as civilian jobs or school that limit how much time they can be away, they sometimes delay attending their MOS school for months. During this time, they still attend weekend drills but can't be promoted until they complete Advanced Training.

How Rank Works

The junior enlisted Soldiers are those that fall below the rank of Sergeant. They encompass four different pay grades, but are broken down into two ranks: Privates and Specialists.

To follow you will find their full title, military rank abbreviation, and pay scale category.

Private (PVT/PV2) E-1 and E-2

Privates provide the basic manpower strength and grade of the Army. A Private has been sworn into the Army and will begin Basic Combat Training. So lowly is the PVT at pay grade E-1, they don't even have a mark of rank on their uniforms. This does not last for long. Within six months or so, the PVT will be promoted to PV2 and wear the chevron displayed above. At any given time, approximately thirty percent of your state's National Guard is made up of Privates. A private's primary role is to carry out orders issued to them to the best of his or her ability. After about a year of drills, you can expect your Private to be promoted to Private First Class (PFC). Privates are promoted based on their maturity, experience, and performance although sometimes they are promoted earlier if there is need.

Private First Class (PFC) E-3

Privates are eligible to be promoted to PFC after one year, or earlier by request of their supervisor. PFCs are given secondary responsibilities such as radio operators or drivers for the platoon leadership. They are still Privates, the lowest of the enlisted ranks, but it's their first ever promotion in the Army and therefore the rank is a lot more gratifying than it would seem. At this point in their career, PFCs will begin to focus on specializing in a particular platoon or organizational function.

Specialist (SPC) E-4

Typically, a Specialist has served a minimum of two years and has completed specific training required for promotion. As their new title would suggest, Specialists are PFCs with enough experience in their MOS to begin acquiring expertise in a particular function of the Army. Specialists are very knowledgeable in their particular MOS and can manage other enlisted Soldiers of lower rank. Most Soldiers reach the rank of SPC as the first term of their enlistment is about to expire. Those who "re-up," or re-enlist, usually stay on to become Noncommissioned Officers.

Noncommissioned Officers (NCOs)

A Noncommissioned Officer (NCO) started out as a junior enlisted Soldier and rose up through the ranks. NCOs are enlisted Soldiers with leadership responsibilities. They are subject matter or MOS experts who have attended Army professional development schools and completed the required coursework to become an NCO.

Corporal (CPL) E-4

While technically the base level of the NCO Corps, the Corporal is seldom an official position within a unit, as the Army recognizes the E-5 pay grade as the first official management position. In the Army, there are two types of E-4s: Corporals and Specialists. Both receive the same pay, but a Corporal is a Noncommissioned Officer. Therefore, the rank Corporal is a leadership designation versus a specialty designation, and is typically awarded to outstanding Specialists who have earned the recognition, but are unqualified to attend the leadership schooling that would allow them to earn the rank of Sergeant.

Sergeant (SGT) E-5

The Sergeant is in direct contact with his assigned group of enlisted Soldiers known as a team. Teams consist of anywhere from six to ten Soldiers, depending on the MOS in which they are working. Two teams generally compose a squad. SGTs are responsible for the motivation, morale, and competency of their troops. The Sergeant trains Soldiers to meet Army standards and makes sure that each member meets the competency requirements of their MOS. Hence, most Sergeants are one of several team leaders within their respective platoons.

Staff Sergeant (SSG) E-6

The duties and responsibilities of the Staff Sergeant closely parallel those of the Sergeant, except that SSGs are typically designated as squad leaders and interact most often with the two SGTs (E-5s) that compose the leadership of the squad. The SSG typically brings four to nine years of experience (depending on the MOS, as some promote faster than others because of need) to the table and is responsible for developing, maintaining, and utilizing the full range of a Soldier's potential. They are in daily contact with a large number of Soldiers and will often have eight to ten Soldiers who work under their direct leadership.

Sergeant First Class (SFC) E-7

In a company organization, the Sergeant First Class is a platoon Sergeant, the second in the platoon's chain of command, behind the platoon leader, a lieutenant. With upwards of three squads and nine NCOs to oversee, the SFC will manage anywhere from a nine to 15-person headquarters staff to a 40-man platoon. Whether they lead a platoon or head up a staff at battalion, the SFC gets the first real taste of administrative responsibility. SFCs on staffs are more focused on administrative responsibilities whereas the platoon Sergeant supervises other Soldiers and takes charge of the platoon in the platoon leader's absence. The SFC generally has several SSGs who work under his or her direct leadership.

Master Sergeant (MSG) E-8

The Master Sergeant serves as the principal administrative NCO at company level or higher. MSGs generally fill instructional or specialized skill positions that demand a higher degree of individual accountability and responsibility as opposed to the normal team system of lower NCOs. Although they share the same pay grade as the First Sergeant, the MSG is focused on administrative duties.

First Sergeant (1SG) E-8

In every company, there is only one senior NCO—the First Sergeant. In the National Guard, 1SGs are very prominent Noncommissioned Officers and tend to stay with their companies for years. The 1SG instructs other Sergeants, advises the company commander, and helps train enlisted

Soldiers. Like the commander, the 1SG is responsible for the welfare of all the Soldiers within a company. Often admirably and sometimes begrudgingly, First Sergeants are referred to as "Top" by their subordinates because of their ascension to the top of the company's food chain.

Sergeant Major (SGM) E-9

The Sergeant Major is often the key enlisted member of the staff elements at battalion and higher levels. The SGM is a subject-matter expert in his or her technical field and often fulfills the duties of the Command Sergeant Major in their absence.

Command Sergeant Major (CSM) E-9

The Command Sergeant Major serves in both a leadership and advisory position within the higher elements of the military organizational structure. The CSM carries out policies and standards on performance, training, appearance, and conduct of enlisted personnel. The CSM gives advice and initiates recommendations to the commander and staff in matters pertaining to enlisted personnel.

Warrant Officers

Most Warrant Officers begin their careers as an enlisted member. To become a Warrant Officer, a Soldier must be in the E-5 pay grade or higher (aviators and some other very technical specialties such as in the medical field are an exception to this rule) and have four to six years experience in an

---

BUT WAIT A SECOND!
Why are there two E-4, two E-8s, and two E-9s?

As if things aren't confusing enough, let me add one more element to the mix. There are certain coveted positions, in both the NCO and Officer ranks, that are leadership positions. Although Soldiers share the same pay grade, they are in different positions. Soldiers are not promoted into leadership positions, they are appointed into leadership positions by their chain of command. Typically, the best are put into leadership roles. Time spent in various leadership positions is a discriminator for promotion boards and career advancement. Enlisted leadership positions include: Master Sergeant, First Sergeant, and Command Sergeant Major. Even though these leaders are in the same pay grade as other NCOs, they wear a different chevron that sets them apart. Platoon Leaders, Executive Officers, Company Commanders, Battalion Commanders, Brigade Commanders, and Division Commanders are all examples of leadership positions. However, Officers wear the insignia of their rank.

MOS related to their Warrant Officer MOS. Every Warrant Officer MOS has a detailed duty description and there are specific prerequisites that must be met or officially waived by the appropriate authorities.

While Commissioned Officers are generalists who are expected to know a little bit about everything, Warrant Officers are specialists who offer expertise in a distinct military technology or capability. A Warrant Officer 1 holds warrants from the Secretary of the Army in positions that warrant the expertise of a commissioned officer. The Warrant Officer Corps comprises less than three percent of the total Army and the Warrant Officer Society tends to be exceptionally close.

Warrant Officer 1 (WO1)

Warrant Officers are single-track specialty Officers, experts, and trainers who operate, maintain, administer, and/or manage the Army's equipment, support activities or technical systems for their entire career e.g., helicopter pilots, advanced computer or weapons systems operators, and logistics controllers.

Chief Warrant Officer 2 (CW2)

A CW2 has met the minimum time in grade as a WO1 (usually two years) and has no negative actions or write-ups against him or her. When promoted to Chief Warrant Officer, they receive their commission from the president and are direct representatives of the president. CW2 is the rank in which a Warrant Officer really begins to hone their skills and expertise in their field. CW2s may be responsible for leading, coaching, training, and/or counseling subordinates. From this point up in rank, all CWOs are commonly referred to as "Chief" (including female Chiefs). Military personnel may also address a CWO as Mister/Mrs./Ms./Miss (Last Name).

Chief Warrant Officer 3 (CW3)

CW3s are both leaders and technical experts who continue to provide valuable skills, guidance, and expertise to company, battalion, or brigade commanders and/or organizations in their particular field. A CW3 is special in that this is the first Warrant Officer rank in which they are granted a commission by the president. As such, in certain circumstances, they may command companies or detachments.

Chief Warrant Officer 4 (CW4)

CW4s are single-specialty, career-track Warrant Officers who are oriented toward progressing within their career field rather than focusing on increased levels of responsibilities or staff duty positions. CW4s are often responsible for the most critical necessities within their units such as finances, logistics, personnel, etc. In aviation, certain CW4s are selected to hold special advisory roles to the battalion commander such as Battalion Safety Officer or Battalion Standardization Instructor Pilot.

Chief Warrant Officer 5 (CW5)

CW5s are the most experienced and proficient Warrant Officers and are equivalent to the full Colonel in their knowledge and experience within their specialty. CWO grades don't always signify differences in job duties but are a reflection of an individual's experience, length of service, and proficiency.

Commissioned Officers

Commissioned Officers hold presidential commissions and are confirmed at their ranks by the Senate. A commission is legally binding and Officers can't just quit the military. If an Officer wants out, he or she must request permission to resign, but only after they have met their obligation. This obligation varies according to the individual Officer's commissioning source. Conversely, they are not employees who can be fired. Both Noncommissioned and Commissioned Officers may be dismissed only if they fail to meet standards. There are specific regulations as to how an Officer or NCO can be dismissed. Soldiers become Commissioned Officers by one of the following methods:

- Graduating from the United States Military Academy, West Point.
- Completing a four-year Reserve Officers' Training Corps (ROTC) program while attending college.
- Completing Officer Candidate School (the Guard of each state operates such a school with students attending classes for two years on drill weekends and during the AT).
- Receiving a direct commission to join one of the professional branches of the Army, such as doctors entering the Medial Corps as Officers.

Second Lieutenant (2LT) O-1

Second Lieutenant is the entry-level rank for Officers and is very close to an apprenticeship role. 2LTs lead a platoon consisting of two or more squads that are comprised of 20 to 50 Soldiers. The Second Lieutenant works closely with the platoon Sergeant. His rank is denoted by a single gold bar.

First Lieutenant (1LT) O-2

After 18 to 24 months of military service, the 2LT is promoted to the rank of First Lieutenant. 1LTs may be selected to be the Executive Officer a.k.a., the XO of a company-sized unit. The XO is the second in command when the company commander is away and is responsible for maintaining training and logistics assignments for the company. During operations, the 1LT may lead a platoon in action if its leader is incapacitated. The First Lieutenant's rank insignia is a single silver bar.

Captain (CPT) O-3

Captains typically command companies within a battalion, where they'll be the sole senior Officer with three to five Lieutenants assisting them or work with several Majors and other Captains as staff Officers for the Colonel who commands the battalion. Captain's insignia are two adjoined silver bars, sometimes referred to as railroad tracks.

Major (MAJ) O-4

Majors are primarily administrative staff Officers in battalions, brigades, and divisions. The battalion Executive Officer functions as second in command for the Lieutenant Colonel battalion commander and is usually focused on personnel and logistics. The Battalion Operations Officer is focused on future and current operational missions. As the first rank of what the Army considers a Field Grade Officer, Majors can be found just about anywhere except at a company. An exception to this is in certain aviation and special operations units. The size of a company may be so large that the position of company commander is reserved for a Major. The Major's rank is denoted by a gold oak leaf.

Lieutenant Colonel (LTC) O-5

Lieutenant Colonels typically command battalion-sized units comprised of 300 to 800 Soldiers, where they will be the sole and only senior Officer. The LTC may also be selected as brigade and task force Executive Officer or Operations Officer. LTC rank insignia is a silver oak leaf.

Colonel (COL) O-6

A Colonel typically commands regimental-sized units comprised of 800 to 1,500 Soldiers. Colonels also can serve as the chief of divisional-level staff agencies. The Colonel's rank insignia is a silver eagle.

Brigadier General (BG) O-7

In the Army, the Brigadier General generally serves as Deputy Commander to the Commanding General for Army divisions. A BG will assist in overseeing the command staff's planning and coordination of a mission. In the Guard, BGs typically command brigades (hence the name Brigadier) composed of about 2,000 or more Soldiers as an element of a division-sized unit, whether it be one of the eight ARNG Infantry Divisions or the Troop Command or group headquarters of a large state. BG rank is indicated by a single silver star.

Major General (MG) O-8

Major Generals in the Army and the Guard typically command division-sized units that are comprised of 10,000 to 15,000 Soldiers. Currently the ARNG has eight divisions, each commanded by an MG. These positions go with the division and not the state. For instance, the 29th Infantry Division (Light) is composed of units primarily from two states, Maryland and Virginia, with the position of Commanding General alternating between them each time a change of command takes place. In most states, the only two-star position is that of the Adjutant General (TAG). By law, each state has a TAG who oversees the work of all state Department of Defense agencies: Army Guard, Air Guard, and state civil service employees that support them. As the senior military Officer of a state or territories military forces, he or she is the principal advisor to the governor in all military matters. There is no "federal standard" that dictates requirements for TAG appointments. Typically, the TAG is a long-serving Air or Army

Guard Officer—but not always. Your state has its own requirements for this top-level appointment. MG rank is indicated by two silver stars.

Lieutenant General (LTG) O-9

On active duty, a Lieutenant General typically commands Corps-sized units that are comprised of two or three divisions. Additionally, many serve in national-command level organizational billets. The Director of the Army National Guard in the National Guard Bureau in Washington, D.C. is a Title 10 AGR Lieutenant General. A LTG's rank is indicated by three silver stars.

★★★★ General (GEN) O-10

A General is the senior level of a Commissioned Officer and will typically have over 30 years experience and service. The General commands all operations that fall within their geographical or command areas. Very few people ever make four star General and none of the 54 states and territories has one for their National Guard forces. The Chief of the National Guard Bureau in Washington was authorized four star General rank by Congress in 2008.

To see how rank connects with the overall organization, check out the following diagram.

Flag Officers

Flag Officers are those in the pay grades of O-7 through O-10 (Brigadier General, Major General, Lieutenant General, General). Less than one percent of career Officers will ever be promoted to Flag Rank. The term General Officer refers to Generals. But while you'll find lots of Generals in the Regular Army, most states and territories will have very few. The reason is that command authority for each only goes as far as the state-line. Since the Guard is a joint force, Generals from either service can and do hold senior leadership positions.

Rank in a Social Setting

It is likely that you will be invited to a few Guard events per

Army Rank and Structure

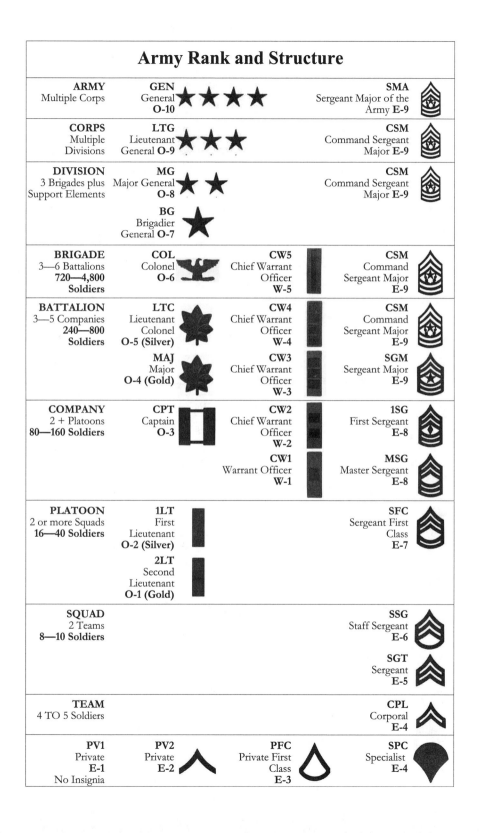

Unit	Officer	Warrant Officer	Enlisted
ARMY Multiple Corps	**GEN** General **O-10**		**SMA** Sergeant Major of the Army **E-9**
CORPS Multiple Divisions	**LTG** Lieutenant General **O-9**		**CSM** Command Sergeant Major **E-9**
DIVISION 3 Brigades plus Support Elements	**MG** Major General **O-8** **BG** Brigadier General **O-7**		**CSM** Command Sergeant Major **E-9**
BRIGADE 3—6 Battalions **720—4,800** **Soldiers**	**COL** Colonel **O-6**	**CW5** Chief Warrant Officer **W-5**	**CSM** Command Sergeant Major **E-9**
BATTALION 3—5 Companies **240—800** **Soldiers**	**LTC** Lieutenant Colonel **O-5 (Silver)** **MAJ** Major **O-4 (Gold)**	**CW4** Chief Warrant Officer **W-4** **CW3** Chief Warrant Officer **W-3**	**CSM** Command Sergeant Major **E-9** **SGM** Sergeant Major **E-9**
COMPANY 2 + Platoons **80—160 Soldiers**	**CPT** Captain **O-3**	**CW2** Chief Warrant Officer **W-2** **CW1** Warrant Officer **W-1**	**1SG** First Sergeant **E-8** **MSG** Master Sergeant **E-8**
PLATOON 2 or more Squads **16—40 Soldiers**	**1LT** First Lieutenant **O-2 (Silver)** **2LT** Second Lieutenant **O-1 (Gold)**		**SFC** Sergeant First Class **E-7**
SQUAD 2 Teams **8—10 Soldiers**			**SSG** Staff Sergeant **E-6** **SGT** Sergeant **E-5**
TEAM 4 TO 5 Soldiers			**CPL** Corporal **E-4**
PV1 Private **E-1** No Insignia	**PV2** Private **E-2**	**PFC** Private First Class **E-3**	**SPC** Specialist **E-4**

year. Whether you are attending an informal family day at your Soldier's armory or a fancy dining out at a hotel, there will be hundreds of people in the room and even if you understand all the nuances of rank, you probably will not have a chance to memorize your Soldier's entire chain of command. And nobody expects you to. Our Soldiers know how to address their fellow Guardsmen and this comes in very handy when we attend events.

When Soldiers are introducing other Soldiers, protocol dictates that junior is introduced to the senior speaking the senior's name first ("Colonel Smith, this is Major Jones, who currently works in the . . . "). At your first event, be prepared for a workout. Your Soldier works with dozens of people—superior, peer, and subordinate—and they will all expect to be introduced to you.

Always remind your Soldier to formally introduce you to his or her co-workers. Upon introduction, offer your hand and repeat their name back so you remember it. If your Soldier doesn't introduce you to somebody, it's

Spoken Forms of Rank in the Army	
Commissioned Officers	
Rank/Service Abbreviation	Address
General (O-10) GEN	"General (last name)"
Lieutenant General (O-9) LTG	
Major General (O-8) MG	
Brigadier General (O-7) BG	
Colonel (O-6) COL	"Colonel (last name)"
Lieutenant Colonel (O-5) LTC	"Colonel (last name)"
Major (O-4) MAJ	"Major (last name)"
Captain (O-3) CPT	"Captain (last name)"

Commissioned Officers	
Rank/Service Abbreviation	Address
First Lieutenant (O-2) 1LT	"Lieutenant (last name)"
Second Lieutenant (O-1) 2LT	"Lieutenant (last name)"
Warrant Officers	
Chief Warrant Officer (all grades) CWO	"Mr./Mrs. (last name)"
Warrant Officer (WO-1) WO	"Mr./Mrs. (last name)"
NCOs and Enlisted Personnel Grades	
Sergeant Major (E-9) SGM	"Sergeant Major"
Master Sergeant (E-9) MSG	"Master Sergeant"
First Sergeant (E-8) 1ST	"First Sergeant"
Sergeant First Class (E-7) SFC	"Sergeant"
Staff Sergeant (E-6) SSG	"Sergeant"
Sergeant (E-5) SGT	"Sergeant"
Corporal (E-4) CPL	"Corporal"
Specialist (E-4) SPC	"Specialist"
Private First Class (E-3) PFC	"Private"
Private (E-1 or E-2) PVT	"Private"

Chaplains

Chaplains are not introduced or addressed by their rank (unless they are in the Navy) they are always called "Chaplain." Their rank may be used in a formal introduction to provide more detail. For example, if they were speaking at an event, the master of ceremonies could say: "Chaplain William Miller, a colonel at the 135th Infantry Regiment, will discuss the benefits of the Strong Bonds program."

probably because they have forgotten their name and don't want to be obvious by staring at their name tag. Don't just jump into conversation to avoid awkwardness. Offer your hand and introduce yourself to the Soldier and his or her spouse.

When you are introduced to your Soldier's superiors, don't worry, you won't be treated like a second-class citizen if you are married to someone of lower (or much lower) rank. The spouses of high-ranking Guardsmen know how important junior-level people are to the organization and they know that your support is vital to long-term retention. You'll typically find that the higher the Soldier's rank, the more comfortable their spouse is in their role. They are seasoned vets and are gracious on every level. I can honestly say that I have never been treated rudely by a superior Officer's spouse. If you meet somebody who treats you poorly or wears their spouses' rank, they have bad manners. Just keep your chin up and be polite and pleasant. This behavior is universally appealing and will impress everyone from Private to General. The beauty of the National Guard is that Soldiers and spouses come from different communities and have different careers. Socializing is much more casual than in the active military. Don't limit your society by only associating with certain people or a certain rank.

Wearing Your Spouse's Rank

While rank garners respect for both Soldier and spouse, you don't have a rank and should never wear your spouse's rank. What this means, basically, is you should not act like a Queen Bee around lower-ranking Soldiers and their spouses. Be proud and supportive of your spouse, but don't use rank as a means to intimidate or ignore other people.

How do *You* Address Military Personnel?

Since you are not in the military and don't have a title, you don't have to address members of the military by their titles. In fact, most members of the military prefer that civilians use their first name. Still, addressing people by their titles is a sign of respect and I would err on the side of formality. Until somebody tells you to call them by their first name, use their title. And when in doubt, always use a title, especially at official military functions. Address military members by their titles:

- In front of other military personnel
- When you are speaking of them in conversations with others
- When you are having a conversation and others are listening
- When introducing them to others

Even if they have asked you to use their first name, only do so when you are speaking with them privately or if you have a longstanding relationship and a precedence of being on a first-name basis (as is the case with many high-ranking Soldiers). If you are personal friends with other Guardsmen and socialize with them unofficially, I would suggest that you greet them using their title. After that, you can call them by their first name.

Other Introductions

At military functions, refer to your spouse by his or her first name. Don't introduce them to others using a title; use their first name. ("Beth, this is my husband, Mike. Mike, this is Beth Smith, Major Smith's wife.") Never refer to him or her in conversation as "Major Smith" or "the Major." However, use your Soldier's title in order to provide context for others. For example, if you are trying to locate your spouse at the armory or are conducting Guard business at a military installment, use their title to help clarify your purpose. ("I'm Beth Smith and I'm here to see Major Smith.")

This is also appropriate for Guard business via e-mail and telephone. If you are contacting a person with whom you are not acquainted, use your spouse's title to provide context. ("This is Beth Smith, Major Smith's wife.") After that, refer to them by their first name.

Shades of Gray

Things get even more confusing when your Soldier's peer gets a promotion. Suddenly, the guy who your husband used to call "Bobby" becomes "Sir." While they shared a rank, they called each other by their first names privately and in appropriate settings (not in front of subordinates). But now that their buddy is their superior, there are new rules. Even if they are great friends, your Soldier will still call rising peers by their title or "Sir/Ma'am" in front of other military personnel. But it is likely that they will address them by their first name during private conversations or if you are socializing as civilians. Even if your Soldier is expected to be promoted soon, he still must show respect by calling people of superior rank by their title in front of other military personnel.

Uniforms

The uniform of the U.S. Army is consistent. Regular Army, National Guard, and Army Reservists all wear the same standard-issue uniforms. The uniform means everything and in the Guard, it is an easy way for regular folks to recognize military members within their communities. People have an immediate reaction to uniformed military personnel and that reaction is, almost always, positive. But sometimes from a spouse's perspective, uniforms can be a bit of a mystery.

There are different uniforms for different duties. There are hats, helmets, belts, boots, badges, ribbons, medals, pins, nameplates, shoulder boards, ropes, and braids. We know that these are not merely accessories that change with fashion cycles, but that each means something, especially to your Soldier. You wonder how they keep track of all of it. But they do. The good news for Guard spouses is that your Soldier knows exactly what to wear, how to wear it, and when to wear it. Even if your civilian husband can't seem to get his head around the no white after Labor Day rule, wears socks with his sandals, or can't put an outfit together to save his life, your Soldier husband always looks dapper and appropriate. Our concerns are simpler:

- Who pays for the uniform?
- How do you take care of the uniform?
- How do you tell rank by uniform?

Who Pays?

As far as costs are concerned, every enlisted Soldier is issued a set of uniforms when they enter Basic Combat Training. Officers pay for their uniforms. The current clothing bag—as the Army calls its list of issued items —includes four sets of the standard camouflage duty uniforms which are called the Army Combat Uniform (ACU). Soldiers are also issued two sets of boots, a belt headgear. Soldiers also receive a set of Class As, the so-called Army Green Service Uniform. This is the dressy green suit that Soldiers wear their ribbons/medals on. There are other, dressier uniforms that are worn for ceremonies and social occasions, but ninety percent of your Soldier's activities are going to be performed in the ACU.

Like any type of clothing, uniforms get worn and need to be replaced. Enlisted Soldiers can turn in heavily worn or damaged uniforms for free replacement. Officers must purchase replacement items. They are readily available both on active military posts and online and you can write the cost off on your taxes. In the long run, however, the best way for your Soldier to save money on replacement items is to stay in shape and take an interest in the care of their uniforms.

Caring for Uniforms

The easiest way to care for ACUs (and all uniforms) is to put your Soldier in charge. Without naming names, I know a certain Soldier who is very picky about how his uniforms are washed. Even though this person could care less about his civilian clothing and throws his stuff on the floor on a daily basis, when it comes to his precious uniforms, all of a sudden he is Mr. Gentle Cycle.

Even though his wonderful, hard-working Laundry Goddess wife tries to help him with this chore, he is completely ungrateful. One time, she dropped all of his ACUs off at the drycleaner to be starched and pressed. Unfortunately, she forgot to pick them up before a drill weekend besides the fact that ACUs are not supposed to be starched. Another time, this selfless woman tried to surprise

---

Hats Off

In June 2011 the soft patrol cap replaced the black beret worn with the Army Combat Uniform. Soldiers will continue to wear black berets with dress uniforms.

him by taking his Dress Blues to the drycleaner. He got really mad at her when he saw all of his ribbons and braidy shoulder-loop things returned in a plastic bag.

And even though this guy never gave any indication that he knew how to set up an ironing board or use an iron, one night she caught him lovingly misting his uniform trousers and ironing meticulous creases into each pant leg. Enough was enough. She got smart and told him, "You are on your own, baby." And that was the last time they fought about his uniforms.

If you are forced at gunpoint to launder your Soldier's uniforms, it really isn't a big deal. The new ACUs are well made and can be thrown in the washer and dryer. Care instructions are inside each garment. We all have our own way of doing laundry. Here's how I do it:

- First, remove ALL of the Velcro patches and clean out all of the pockets (especially the pen holder slots and cell phone/Blackberry pocket! I have put my husband's Blackberry through the washer before. Not good.).
- Throw them in the washing machine on a cold temperature with regular detergent (don't use any kind of bleach or laundry detergent with bleach in it). Don't mix ACUs in with your regular laundry because the Velcro loops may snag other clothing. Wash uniforms separately.
- Dry them in the dryer on a regular cycle.
- Remove them promptly so they don't wrinkle.
- Hang them on a high-quality coat hanger. Put patches back in place.
- No ironing required. In fact—it's not even allowed anymore. I'm sure it is for national security reasons, but no matter because you're off the hook.
- And one more thing you may not know: not only does your Soldier know how to launder his own uniform, he also knows how to make a bed with hospital corners. They learned these skills, and many others that can lighten your load, at Basic Training. Not that they'll ever admit it.

Dress uniform jackets, slacks, and skirts (Class As and Dress/Mess Blues) can't be laundered at home and should NOT be dry cleaned unless there are stains that can't be removed by spot cleaning. Dry cleaning is very hard on the satin jacket lapels and ideally, dress uniforms should only be professionally cleaned every three years. However, ties and shirts may be sent to the drycleaner after each wear. The easiest way to keep coats and slacks fresh and clean is to spot clean any stains with a damp, clean cloth. Remove belts and braces and keep them hung up, unbuttoned, on a high-quality, wooden or padded hanger. Give them a rest between wears and leave plenty of space around the uniform when hanging. To remove wrinkles, hang them in the bathroom and use the shower to create steam. It is best not to iron the uniform, but if you must, place a cotton cloth between the iron and the fabric. You can mist them lightly with a fabric spray in between wears. When it comes time for tri-annual cleaning, your Soldier will need to remove absolutely everything from them. Cleaning expenses for uniforms are tax deductible.

These Boots Were Made for Scuffin'

I have to say that I really miss the old black boots. They could be polished and repaired and they always looked sharp. They lasted forever and it gave the corner of their closet that cool retro smell. The new boots, while not high maintenance as far as spit-shining, lack that certain *j'ne se qua*. No matter how carefully your Soldier cares for them, they show wear easily and they won't look new after a month of wear. Your Soldier should care for them as you would a pair of suede shoes. Introduce them to the merits of a hard-bristled suede brush. This will remove dirt and fluff up the nap.

Perfection is a Spray Away

While the boots that your Soldier wears most of the time can look pretty shabby pretty fast, you can make up for this by springing for the black patent leather dress shoes (pumps for women) that are worn with the dress uniforms. Your Soldier may opt to wear his or her own black leather lace-ups or pumps, which is perfectly acceptable, with their dress uniforms, but I would suggest investing in a pair of the patent leather styles available on any military base or online. Care is easy. You spray them with glass cleaner, wipe them off with a paper towel, smile at your crystal clear reflection, and send them on their way. These are not issued by the Army, but are well worth the fifty bucks. It may seem odd to see grown men wearing patent leather shoes, but these are the same style that civilians wear with tuxedos and are stylish and classic. Most importantly, they will last for years and years.

Equipment versus Uniform

In addition to uniforms, Soldiers are issued equipment. Backpacks, fold-up shovels, helmets, webbed-gear, gloves of all thickness and color, and countless types and sizes of bags. Most of which finds its way into your garage and car trunks. Warning: Don't ever throw anything out. It may look like junk or garage sale material but know that somewhere, somehow, somebody knows what equipment has been issued to your Soldier. And even though it seems like stuff that just sits there, somebody may ask for it back. When we moved from Minnesota to Georgia, some of Jon's stuff got lost in the shuffle. A few months later, we received a list of items that needed to be returned to the Minnesota National Guard. After finding what we could in our garage, we took the list to a local military supply store and replaced missing items. Anything that we could not account for, we paid for. I would strongly suggest that you give your Soldier a dedicated space for their equipment and uniforms. If you have been in the Guard family for years, you know as well as I do that the green stuff can take over your house.

Ribbons

The same ribbons that are an unending source of curiosity for civilians are, more often than not, a source of stress for Soldiers. Ribbons must be worn in a very specific manner and as your Soldier's career progresses, they will change over and over again. Thanks to technology, "ribbon management" has become easier. If your Soldier's ribbons suffer from seatbelt trauma, or you accidentally lose them, federal issue replacements can be ordered online. Your Soldier can save a lot of time figuring out his/her ribbon arrangements through the cool website www.ezrackbuilder.com. He or she can organize their ribbons and order necessary items direct from sister site www.USAMilitaryMedals.com. It should be noted that all states issue their own state ribbons expressly for Guard service. These always follow federal issued ribbons in precedence order. If they are lost or federally damaged replacements can be purchased through channels within the Guard supply chain.

How to Tell Rank on a Uniform

In the earlier part of this chapter, we discussed the rank structure and reviewed all the chevrons and insignias. Now it's time for the fun part, learning how to tell rank at a glance. To tell a Soldier's rank when they are wearing their ACUs, look at the front center of their chest where you will see an embroidered rank insignia or chevron. If the Soldier is a Private, or E-1, they will have a blank cloth patch that will soon be replaced by an E-2 chevron. An interesting note, an Army chaplain's pin-on insignia is the only branch insignia authorized on an ACU.

The ASU

When a Soldier wears his or her Army Service Uniform (ASU), what most people call Dress Blues, there are several ways to tell a Soldier's rank and status. Male Commissioned Officers will have a gold band running down the side of their trouser legs. Both male and female Commissioned Officers will wear their rank insignia on vertical shoulder boards that lay across the seam of their shoulders. Male and female Noncommissioned Officers will have gold service stripes on the outside of their left sleeve. Junior enlisted personnel wear rank insignia between shoulder seam and the elbow on both sleeves.

It's Not Easy Being Green

As this book goes to press, the Army is implementing a phase out of the Class A Green Uniform. Although AR 670-1 hasn't been officially changed, it is likely that the wear-out date will be 2014. Dress Blues will become the new Army Service Uniform (ASU) and will be worn year-round. (Previously, Blues were reserved for ceremonies and formal occasions.)

The new uniform will have the same overall look as the current Blues, but it will have a more tailored fit. A necktie will be worn under the ASU for everyday wear. A white shirt paired with a bowtie will be worn under the ASU for formal occasions. Basically, most Soldiers will own two uniforms: the ACU ("camo" uniform) and the ASU ("blue" uniform) which makes telling rank by uniform even simpler!

Wrap Up

- You don't have to be an expert in rank. Your job is to support your Soldier in the best way that you possibly can. However, understanding the general roles and responsibilities within the Guard organization will help you identify key players and see how your Soldier fits into the big picture.

- We are all proud of our Soldiers, and every Soldier's job is mission critical. Rank isn't about fancy titles and who bosses who around. Rank is about making sure that the job gets done. Rank is about keeping people as safe as possible and there can't be a military without clearly defined rank.

- The Guard matches an individual's skill sets and experience to mission critical, measurable actions. Rank provides the means to organize moving parts into a lean, mean, fighting machine.

- Whether you are attending an informal family day at your Soldier's armory or a fancy dining out at a hotel, there will be hundreds of people in the room and even if you know everything there is to know about rank, you will really have to be on your game to identify your Soldier's entire chain of command. That's not necessary. But if you want to know more about the person you are talking to, a quick glance to the shoulder will tell you a lot about them.

Why is the Flag Patch Backward?

"It's not!" your Soldier insists. But it sure looks backwards to you. Here's why:

The flag is worn on the right shoulder because in the military, the place of honor is to a military member's right. The full-color, cloth replica is worn so that the star field faces forward or to the flag's own right. When worn in this manner, the flag is facing to the observer's right and gives the effect of the flag flying in the breeze as the wearer moves forward. The rule dates back to the Army's early history, when both mounted cavalry and infantry units would designate a standard bearer who carried the Colors into battle. As he charged, his forward momentum caused the flag to stream back. Since the Stars and Stripes are mounted with the canton closest to the pole, that section stayed to the right, while the stripes flew to the left.

Adapted from Rod Powers, "Why is the U.S. flag worn "backwards" on the uniform?" Accessed August 20, 2010
http://usmilitary.about.com/od/jointservices/a/hooah.htm

- While you are not required to address military personnel by their titles, it is a sign of respect. A retired Colonel put it this way, "Until someone tells you to call them by their first name, use their title. When talking to someone individually, use whatever they tell you to use. When other military personnel are listening, use their title. Always use a formal title when talking to anyone if there are any doubts. It eliminates confusion and is a sign of respect for others."
- Don't refer to your Soldier by their title in front of other military personnel. Call him or her by their first name.
- There are many rules and regulations when it comes to uniforms. The good news is that this isn't your lane. Your Soldier knows what to wear, how to wear it, and when to wear it.
- Put money in your budget to replace worn uniforms and footwear. Soldiers should always look squared away. Keep the receipts for any uniform expenses including dry cleaning. Any purchases made from your personal account can be written off on your taxes. Clothing purchased with a government clothing allowance, can't be written off.
- Telling rank by uniform depends on which uniform Soldiers are wearing. Ninety percent of the time, Soldiers wear ACUs. Rank is worn in the middle of their chest.
- The Army has announced the new Army Service Uniform (ASU) and is working on the rewrite of AR 670-1. Basically, Dress Blues will replace Class A uniforms.

Chapter 5

The Promotion System

Promotions: A Big-Picture View

Promotion is important to your Soldier because it validates all of the hard work they have put into their Guard career and shows that their chain of command sees their potential. Your Soldier wants to be challenged and promotion means new responsibilities and challenges. For you, promotion means meeting new members of the Guard family. It means more visibility within the Guard organization. But wait a second . . . I'm forgetting something . . . What could it be? Oh, yes, of course, promotion means more money. And even though our Soldiers are not in it for the money, let's be honest, we all like money. Some of us even love money.

And financial security is important. Whatever you do with your Guard income in the short-term, whether you invest it, save it, or use it to make ends meet, everybody appreciates a pay increase. In the long-term, the higher the rank, the higher the retirement benefit. This directly impacts your family. Promotions are important to all of us.

Guard promotions are very complex. There are numerous policies, regulations, and requirements; to explain the process in full detail would be giving you much more information than you need to know. There are differences in the way enlisted versus Officers are promoted. And there are subtle differences in the way that each state organization runs promotions. And just when you think you understand how things work, they change! But let me start by saying this, you don't have to do anything during the promotion process. There are ways that you can support your Soldier before, during, and after he or she is considered for promotion, and we will get to that later. For now, just know that it is your Soldier's responsibility to manage their military career. If you want to know how the promotions process will work for your Soldier, ask them! As complex as the process seems to us, our Soldiers get how the system works and if they don't they can easily get the information from their superiors. Things change constantly in the military, but there are no secrets. Information about promotions is documented in official Department of Defense publications which are available online at Guard Knowledge Online https://gko.ngb.army.mil. So, if your Soldier can't answer your questions, these documents can. I hope that this chapter will answer some of your most basic questions.

The Real Deal

To get promoted, Soldiers need to be at the top of their game. They need to be squared away and have a proven track record of performance. In addition, they must show potential. Measuring both of these attributes is difficult. As we discussed during Chapter 4, the Army isn't a subjective organization. It relies on a strict rank system to get the job done and keep Soldiers safe. The promotion process reflects this. If it seems like your Soldier has to jump through a hundred hoops to reach the next level, that's because it is true. Each Soldier must meet strict and specific criteria to be eligible for promotion.

But eligibility does not guarantee anything. Soldiers must meet or exceed the requirements of their current grade to be promoted to the next one. And even if they are a stellar performer and have checked off all the requirements on the list, Soldiers (above base ranks) must compete against qualified peers within their same career field, within their state, to secure a slot. In some cases, Officers are required to compete at the Department of the Army level.

Base Level Promotions

Base level promotions (from PV2 to E-4, from WO1 to CW2, from 2LT to 1LT) are decentralized. If a Soldier performs well and has completed the required Time in Grade and Time in Service, the unit or company has promotion authority. There isn't a quota that dictates the number of Soldiers that can be promoted to the next highest grade. For the most part, if a Soldier meets the promotion criteria and has put in his or her time, they will be promoted automatically along with their peers. Of course, the Soldier must be in good standing. For example, if a Soldier is flagged on his or her APFT, is on weight control, or is pending adverse actions, they will not be promoted.

Time in Service/Time in Grade

Time in Service (TIS) refers to how long the Soldier has been in the Army (the clock begins the day a Soldier reports for Basic Training). Some promotions have a TIS requirement. Time in Grade (TIG) refers to the minimum amount of time a Soldier must spend in their current rank to be promoted to the next rank. They must meet this time requirement to get the training and experience they need to succeed at the next level and give leadership a big enough window to assess their skills and determine if they are ready for promotion.

Supply and Demand

For all other grades, the promotion system is driven by supply and demand. Generally speaking, the demand for Soldiers in every pay grade and MOS is determined from the top down. Every year the Army decides how many people can be promoted into each grade and MOS. These numbers are passed down to the Guard Bureau, which in turn passes the numbers down to each state. Each state is given authorization (and funding) to staff a certain number of part-time Soldiers and a certain number of full-time Soldiers. The number of Soldiers that your state will be authorized to have on their payroll depends largely on the number and types of units in your state a.k.a., force structure. And of course, the larger the total size of Guard Soldiers that your state chooses to maintain, the more opportunities there are for advancement.

Even if your state has the authority to promote Soldiers, there must be a valid vacancy for them to be promoted into. And Soldiers must be qualified for the particular position in which they are being promoted (meaning, for example, an artillery SSG can't be promoted to fill an infantry SSG position). Thus, even if the supply of Officers eligible for promotion is high, individual states are limited in the number of Soldiers they can promote by the number of vacant positions they have. For example, if a Colonel retires, this will open a Colonel vacancy for a Lieutenant Colonel to fill. This in turn will open a Lieutenant Colonel position for a Major to be promoted into and so on. It is like a reverse domino effect; for your Soldier to be promoted, others must fall forward and be promoted into the next grade or retire, leaving vacant slots to fill. One thing to keep in mind is that the Guard organization is like a pyramid; there are many more Lieutenants than Colonels. There are many more Sergeants than Sergeant Majors and so on. As a rule, the higher the rank, the fewer slots available. As your Soldier rises up the ranks, the demand (or number of slots) decreases as the supply (qualified Soldiers) increases.

Competition

We want the Guard to be competitive. We want the best qualified Soldiers to rise to the top. But getting to the top isn't easy. For one, you can't skip any levels in the military. A Soldier must climb up the ladder one rung (or rank) at a time and serve a minimum TIS or TIG at every rank to even be considered for promotion. But even if they have served the minimum amount of time, very few Soldiers are actually promoted as soon as they are eligible for promotion. Most Soldiers will be promoted in the average amount of time that a Soldier must spend in grade to be promoted.

Commissioned Officer Promotions

The ARNG uses two systems to promote Officers. The first is the mandatory promotion selection board process otherwise known as the Department of the Army (DA) Reserve Component board. This board process is mandated by section 14101(a) of Title 10 United States Code. The second system is the vacancy promotion system. This system is addressed in section 307 of Title 32 United States Code. It is important to remember that the appointment of Officers in the National Guard is reserved as a right of the states by the U.S. Constitution article 1, section 8, clause 16. As such, the determination of who will be promoted rests with the TAG of the state or his or her designated subordinate commanders.

To be considered for a DA board promotion, an Officer must complete their minimum TIS/TIG and submit a packet according to the requirements/deadlines set forth by both the Army and their state Guard organization. Packets include recent OERs (Officer Evaluation Reports) which are really like performance reviews, an official photograph of the Soldier normally taken at a photo studio on a military installation, appropriate forms that list awards/recognitions, military education, and civilian education. Soldiers (both enlisted and Officers) must have an updated physical on file. After submitting a packet, Officers will compete against their qualified peers to be selected for promotion.

Enlisted Promotions

Enlisted promotions are filled through the state's Enlisted Promotion System (EPS). Each Soldier eligible for promotion (based on TIS/TIG requirements) will submit an official packet on or before the state's annual promotion board date. The packet includes a point worksheet that documents awards, training, and educational data. It also rewards points for specific discriminators. In addition, a Soldier's records will appear before a formal board who will evaluate past performance and potential. All of this information, and more, is put into the Soldier's packet.

Note: although promotions for Active Guard Reserve Soldiers (both Officers and enlisted) still follow the processes above, there are some key differences in how these promotions happen and some additional hoops to jump through. If your Soldier is AGR, ask them to tell you how it works.

The Packet: Promoting the Product

Ah yes, the packet. Oh mighty burner of the midnight oil. Oh creator of a thousand errands. Oh great thief of family time. How you will come to know the illustrious Guard packet. On a positive note, there is change on the horizon that will help reduce the hard copy promotion packet. Packets are the way that our Soldiers promote themselves in a standardized, subjective manner. They are, really, the advertisement. The required content of a packet for both enlisted and Officer promotions are dictated by the Guard and instructions must be followed to a "T." Your Soldier must work within the constraints of the system to convince a selection board that they should be promoted. Packets include many, many components. But basically, all of these components work toward the same end, to show that the Soldier has the magic that will help secure a promotion:

- Proven Performance—they have mastered the requirements of their current grade.
- Promising Potential—they have the potential to meet the requirements of the next grade and beyond.

It is vital that your Soldier put together the best product possible. This takes time, a lot of time. If your Soldier is submitting a packet, it will take time to coordinate all of the required information. This effort does not only involve filling out forms, but collecting specific information from specific resources. While much of the packet can be compiled remotely, it will take some running around to get all of the information. They will have to have a current physical on record. If they are missing any OERs, they will have to track them down or contact the appropriate persons to write them. If they need to get their picture taken, they will have to schedule this with the appropriate people. Make sure your Soldier does not procrastinate. Most Soldiers start preparing their packet a few months in advance because it takes this long to get it pulled together. Be aware that all of this work is done on your Soldier's own time, not over drill weekends. Give your Soldier the time they need to get this done. It isn't a simple process, but it is important to both you and your Soldier.

The Product

One thing that I know for sure is that a packet is useless if you don't have a good product to promote. Your Soldier is that product. If they want to increase their chance of being promoted, they must be constantly working toward that goal. They must be in shape. They must have completed their civilian and military educational requirements. They must perform for their chain of command. Scrambling to make the grade two months before promotion boards are held is a waste of time. If you have ever painted a room, you know that most of the time and effort is spent doing prep work. You have to scrape the walls, fill the holes, tape off the baseboards, and apply a quality primer. If you don't do all of these things, the paint job will just be so-so. At first glance, it may look good. But upon closer inspection, you will see the flaws. And if you compare it to a well-prepared room, the flaws become magnified. It is the same way in the Army. The lion's share of work is completed before the promotion packet is assembled. Promotions are not about packets. Promotions are about the Soldier. Great Soldiers are always at the ready.

If your Soldier wants to be at the ready for promotion, it can mean little things like making sure they are always well-groomed (thus the twice-a-month haircut in many of our budgets!). They need to make sure their uniform is in tip-top condition and that they look the way people expect a Soldier to look. Yes, that's right—looks matter. And the photo included in a packet isn't just a formality. People on promotion boards will look at these carefully to see if the Soldier looks squared away. They need to look fit. They need to look sharp. And, their tie needs to be on straight! If you want to know how a Soldier should look, check out the highest ranking Officer at the next Guard event. I have yet to meet an overweight or unkempt General or CSM! They are always the very model.

This is where you can really help your Soldier. Let me put this in civilian terms. If you are looking for a job, you know how much work is involved in acing out your competition and getting that offer letter. You have made phone calls, customized your resume, gone on interviews, and worked hard to show a future employer that you are the one for the job. When you finally start your new job, you are excited and energized. You are ready to take on the world. You probably have about 100 different initiatives that you are ready to tackle. You want to be a stellar performer and show your potential to move up within the organization. You dress professionally and look your best. You show up early and leave late. You start off strong and get a lot done. And everybody notices. They praise your work and reward you with a great performance appraisal, more responsibility or more flexibility.

At that point, you have a choice to make: you can either (1) rest on your laurels and hope that your early efforts will be remembered down the road when it comes time for your salary review or (2) continue performing at your maximum capacity everyday. Maybe you start getting to the office a bit later everyday. Maybe you take a long lunch hour more than you should. Maybe you take a vacation when your team needs you to work on an important proposal. You decide that you are not going to attend extra social events (after all, they are not mandatory). Or you stop dressing to the nines and decide that business casual means wrinkled pants or a jacket that has seen better days. You decide that you are going to relax a bit and be like everybody else. I can honestly say that I have done both. I have kicked it in and taken names. And I have gotten comfortable and done the minimum amount of work to get the job done. And guess what? When I kept the intensity level up, I was rewarded. When I didn't, I stagnated.

The same thing goes for your Soldier's Guard career. If they want a good product to promote, the status quo is unacceptable. There is no getting comfortable. And you must be prepared for this. If your Soldier comes home from a long day of work and needs to go for a run, it isn't about getting away from the kids or having "me time." It is about keeping physically fit so he or she can get the highest scores possible on the APFT. If they need to invest in a new uniform because their current one is starting to look shabby, put it in your budget. If they have reached the rank of LTC or MSG, they may decide that they want to invest big bucks into a set of Mess Blues to show that they are in it for the long haul. If they need to finish their college degree at night, it isn't going to be a cakewalk, but it needs to be done. If a superior Officer needs them to take the heat from somebody so they can focus on putting out a fire elsewhere, they need to do it. The best thing you can do to help get your Soldier promoted is ask them what they think they need to do to stand out. Have them be specific. Discuss what, exactly, their action plan is and how it will affect your family. And, if your response is, "Whatever you need to do, I'm here to support you," I commend you.

Miles and Miles

One thing worth noting is that, in some cases, a Soldier will be offered a promotion to a position that is far from home. They don't have to take the position, but for Officers, this may mean they will be, in essence, put back to the bottom of the promotion list. When promotions are being decided, the powers-that-be are not referencing each Soldier's mailing address. People are matched with openings. Believe me, none of us are thrilled when our Soldiers drill far from home, but if you want your Soldier to be competitive, the best strategy is to be flexible. I know plenty of Soldiers that drill far from their homes because they didn't want to limit their opportunity for advancement. This means that they will spend a lot of time on the road and spend nights away from home. Hopefully, in time, they may be able to drill closer to home. This is definitely a decision that you and your Soldier should make together.

For enlisted Soldiers, at the beginning of every promotion cycle, Soldiers may specify a mileage declamation in their packet. For example, if a Soldier states "I will not travel more than 100 miles from my home of record," they will not be offered available positions at those units (some states break their organization into territories from which Soldiers can choose those areas they will accept assignments). For enlisted Soldiers, turning away a position far from home does not kick them down to the bottom of list. However, if a Soldier declines a position within 50 miles of their home of record, they will be removed from the list. AGR Soldiers need to be available for all state assignments and can't take a mileage declamation.

Market Leader

Once in awhile, you will meet an Officer or NCO who seems very young for their rank. How does this happen? Well, they are the market leaders. And even though the Guard's rank and promotion system is set in stone, that does not mean that there are not ways to reward exceptional performers.

Market leaders work within the system to create innovative, efficient ways to accomplish tasks and solve problems. Even though Soldiers can't skip ranks and promotions are not subjective, a very small number of Soldiers help influence the competitive climate through exceptional performance. These are the people who are promoted as soon as they are eligible. And, in a few cases, these high-achievers get promoted below the zone over and over again. How do they do this? Well, they never get comfortable. They understand that every task performed, no matter how menial or irrelevant it seems, is a chance to show their potential. They also have an uncanny ability to exceed the requirements of their current grade while anticipating what they need to do to make it up the next rung of the ladder. Even when you think they are a known entity, they are constantly assessing their offerings against the marketplace and coming up with new ways to improve the Guard organization so it can attract bright, energetic recruits. They are innovators and really stand out. They know how to align their skill set with the set requirements of their rank against the evolving needs of the Guard organization.

Most importantly, they show initiative. If they need to kick it up a notch, they do it. Maybe they raise their hand and volunteer for a specific mission. Maybe they put on their running shoes and push the bread basket away so they can stay in shape. Or, they increase their exposure to their superiors by putting in countless volunteer hours for a professional organization. Whatever needs to be done, they do it. No excuses. That is why they not only set the competitive bar, but continue to ace out their competition. They have, in essence, shortened their time to market. If you ever meet a Guardsman who seems young for their rank, this may be how they beat the system. And I can guarantee you that behind every one of these market leaders are a supportive and engaged family that has made many sacrifices to support them. They are the ultimate product. And you are the one who gives them the motivation and support they need to rise to the top.

How Do You Find Out if Your Soldier Has Been Promoted?

For Officer promotions, every state has their own way of doing things. Typically, however, Officers considered for promotion by a DA board will receive a letter in the mail (usually within a month) informing them whether or not they have been selected. Bear in mind that because the Constitution reserves the right to promote Officers in the Guard up to the states, selection for promotion by the DA board does not necessarily mean the Officer is going to be promoted. There are various reasons why an Officer that is selected by the DA board may not be promoted in their state. For example, there may not be a position at the higher grade for which the Officer is qualified. In this case, the Officer has the option to transfer to the Individual Ready Reserve (IRR) and accept the promotion. The decision to do this must be weighed carefully as it would mean leaving the Guard and going into an inactive status. If the Officer isn't selected for promotion by the DA board, the letter will include very basic information but does not provide any reasoning behind the decision.

For enlisted promotions, the notification process varies from state-to-state. However, by regulation, every state must have a procedure in place to contact individuals and solicit their acceptance for vacancies. The enlisted point system results in a clear list of Soldiers who can be promoted. The list is maintained by State Headquarters and is updated constantly. The promotion list is required to be posted on each unit's bulletin board. However, the list changes every day and the copy displayed may be outdated. The full-time folks at the armory have access to the updated list on a daily basis and if your Soldier wants to know where they are on the list, they can get this information easily.

Typically, if a unit has a vacancy, the number one Soldier (in the appropriate grade) will be contacted by the Promotion Manager from State

Headquarters and offered the promotion. Sometimes, the unit will be given the Soldier's name and they will contact the Soldier directly. Once this contact is made and the position is accepted, the Soldier is promoted. From that point, most headquarters will publish orders which will be sent to the gaining unit. The Soldier will be officially promoted at the first weekend drill information by new command. Some states allow the losing unit to promote the Soldier at the last weekend drill before he or she departs for the new assignment. When the order is cut, it will go into the system and pay will be updated. The great news is that this happens quickly, especially if a Soldier is promoted in theater.

The Verdict

More often than not, you will know whether your Soldier has been promoted or not before the letter arrives through the grapevine. Your Soldier will probably find out the outcome from his friends and colleagues in the Guard. This is a very touchy subject and requires a lot of sensitivity. If your Soldier wasn't selected for promotion, you may be upset about it. Especially if some of his or her peers were selected. You may feel defensive. You may not understand why some people were promoted and others were not. It is natural to feel like this. We all think our Soldiers are the best, as it should be! But don't crab to your Soldier about it. Don't make them feel worse than they already do. Just let them know that you are there to help them for the next go-around. There are many reasons why some Soldiers are promoted and others are not. But respect the rank system and know that everything happens for a reason. Be gracious to those who were promoted. Keep your sense of humor! Is there anything more boring than people who take things so seriously all of the time? A sense of humor and mature, gracious manners always disarm the competition. Move onward and upward. Remember, there is a lot of competition in the Guard.

It's Official!

If your Soldier was selected for promotion—congratulations! You will be officially informed by letter, but again, you will probably hear the good news well before it arrives. If your Soldier is promoted, you should be very proud indeed. It is customary to host a party in their honor. Invite your civilian friends and ask your Soldier to give you the names and addresses of Guard friends and their spouses. You may also want to consider co-hosting a party with other Soldiers who have been promoted to the same grade level. Invite people of any rank. Even if people are unable to attend, they will appreciate being included. The promotion ceremony will be part of the regular drill weekend. Some promotions are done during the unit's formation. Other promotions (for higher ranks) may be done in a separate ceremony.

Either way, you should plan on attending to show your support. As soon as your Soldier has his or her federal recognition orders in hand, they may start using their new title. Their pay raise should be seen the month after the federal recognition order is delivered to the pay office for processing.

Spouse Etiquette and Promotions

How you or your Soldier conduct yourselves around promotions is important in both the short-and long-term. The classiest way to handle promotions is not to mention anything about promotions to other Guard spouses. It is just rude and the civilian equivalent of asking what somebody's salary is. It is also assuming that all spouses are involved in all the details of their Soldier's Guard career. That is simply not the case.

Support your Soldier as he or she improves their chances to be selected the next time around. They have probably heard some feedback from their chain of command about what they need to do to improve their chances for promotion next time. For example, if your Soldier needs to attend professional advancement schools or complete more training, encourage them to enroll and complete the next level of their military education requirements at the first opportunity. They may need to improve their scores on the APFT. In the higher ranks, Soldiers may want to consider getting a master's degree. There are many programs geared toward Soldiers. My husband completed his undergraduate degree through an online program that was coordinated with our state's education office.

Be truly happy for people who rise up in the ranks. They have earned it. But know that as your Soldier moves up in rank, you become more visible within the organization. Even though you must act in a way that is appropriate for your spouse's rank, don't alienate yourself from other Soldiers and their families because you have enough friends already or are most comfortable interacting with your Soldier's peer group. You and your

Soldier have invested years of time and energy into their Guard career. You have made sacrifices. He or she has made sacrifices. Some have even risked their lives. After all of this, you want to be able to maintain your life-long membership in the Guard family. Don't ever forget what it was like to be at the bottom. These people and their families are now your brothers and sisters, people who will greet you with open arms, a warm smile, and a lot of stories to share at events years from now. Reach out to them.

Wrap Up

- Whether your Soldier is an NCO or Officer, the promotion process is extremely complicated. However, it is also very straightforward. Your Soldier knows how promotions work, and if they don't, there are plenty of resources available to walk them through the process.
- The promotion process is similar for enlisted and Officers. Basically, Soldiers must meet Army requirements, put together a packet that includes very specific items, and compete against their qualified peers.
- With the exception of base-level promotions, there must be slots open for promotions to be offered. The Army decides exactly how many enlisted/Officers can be promoted per grade and MOS. Even if Soldiers are put on the promotion list, it may take awhile for their official promotion.
- If your Soldier isn't promoted, support him or her as they try and improve their chance for selection the next time around. Respect the rank system and be gracious to those who have been promoted.
- If your Soldier is promoted . . . Congratulations! Throw a party to honor their accomplishment. Just be extra sensitive to any friends whose Soldiers were not promoted.
- During the promotion process, you don't have to do anything or provide any information. Just support your Soldier before, during, and after the process and leverage your new understanding of how promotions work to help them in any way you can.

Chapter 6

What if your Spouse
is the Company Commander?

(Note to Readers: although there are female company commanders, the reality is that 88% of ARNG Officer spouses are women. To improve readability, this information is written specifically for them.)

If your husband is the company commander, you probably have some experience with Guard life already. As a Lieutenant, he served as a platoon leader within a company. It's likely that you have met other Guard spouses at an annual picnic or holiday celebration. We learned in "The Company Line" how the food chain works and you know that the company is where it all happens. Everything you have learned thus far will come in handy when your spouse becomes a company commander.

Being in command is an honor and it will be one of the highlights of your husband's career. But with the excitement comes increased responsibility and accountability. Your husband has to take care of an entire company of Soldiers and has to answer to a lot of people in his chain of command. A successful command is vital to future career advancement and you need to prepare yourself for the extra time that the position will require of him. Sometimes it is frustrating, and I would be a liar if I said I never complained about the extra hours, but you must step up to the plate and support your husband as much as you possibly can. The commander is the first one in and the last one out on drill weekends. In addition, he will spend extra time on evenings and weekends keeping up with paperwork, attending leadership meetings, or just fielding phone calls from his NCOs and Lieutenants. And if people can't get a hold of him, they will call you.

In the Guard, a lot of action is packed into a small amount of time. Efficiency is the name of the game. When you have a big meeting at work, it takes weeks to prepare for it. You have to schedule the meeting, invite the VIPs, book the conference room, order the bagels, and make sure the technical props are ready to go. Then there is the presentation that you have to get together and all the people who have to give you their input and feedback before you have a final product. And when that's all done, you have to figure out what, exactly, you are going to say. Even if you delegate half of these to-dos, this takes time too. And just when you have everything ready to go, something changes. Or somebody who needs to be there, can't be there and it's back to the drawing board. And don't forget that while you are doing all of this, you still have to do your job. If you procrastinate, or just try and wing it, your disorganization will show and things will inevitably fall through the cracks. If you are organized, you will shine and your meeting will be productive. But being organized means working overtime. And the company commander definitely works overtime.

Drill weekends are like extreme business meetings. The company commander's number one priority is to maximize face-to-face time with the Soldiers. Soldiers are at drill to train—not to stand in a corner while the Officers and NCOs figure out what to do next. As a result, leadership often meets after hours on drill weekends, to debrief the day's activities and start short-term planning the next month's drill and long-term planning for any special missions. (Dirty little secret: after hours is seldom enough so don't be surprised if it's a weeknight on the run-up to the weekend or the dreaded "second weekend.")

Although there is a lot of extra work involved with company command, don't get so wrapped up in that aspect of the job that you don't savor the experience. The company that your husband commands will hold a special place in both of your hearts forever. What used to look like an armory made of bricks and mortar will start to feel like a second home. When you are married to the company commander, you will spend more time at the armory. You will notice how hard the Soldiers work to keep the floors spotless. You will see how the cooks pull out all the stops when family members attend a special event. You will meet the NCOs and Lieutenants who work with your husband and get to know their spouses. You will meet battalion leadership from time-to-time and start to see how things operate. You may meet former commanders and their wives and feel that you are part of a very special legacy. Best of all, you will meet fresh-faced young Soldiers with big smiles and great manners. The chivalry and work ethic that they demonstrate make you forget that some of these Soldiers are barely out of high school. You will be humbled because even though you can't seem to remember anybody's name, they all remember you. If you show up from time-to-time during a drill weekend, everybody will go out of their way to make sure you and your kids are comfortable. After all the hard work is done and your husband's command is over, you will look back on the experience fondly and miss that armory and those people.

Your Wish is My Command

Every company has a commander. The company commander does exactly what the title implies: he or she oversees the entire company according to Army standards. It is the commander's job to make sure the company is mission-ready—not just for a specific mission by a certain deadline, but for any and all missions that may arise without warning. This is the biggest challenge of all, to be prepared at a moment's notice to do whatever the governor or president needs to be done, whenever they need it done. All of our Soldiers are trained in their specialty and can anticipate long-term deployments. But when two feet of snow fall in two days in Denver or tornados rip through Lady Lake, Florida—they have to be ready to move out. Now! The commander is the one who orchestrates this at the company level.

The company commander is always an Officer and almost always a Captain. Armed with what he learned as a Lieutenant/platoon leader, a Captain takes these skills to a higher level when leading a company. In addition to keeping tabs on his or her direct reports, the commander is responsible for the maintenance and accountability of those items assigned to the company, as well as the maintenance of company strength retention, recruiting, morale, and family readiness efforts. The time spent as a company commander (typically between 18 and 24 months) goes by fast. This is a fast-paced, high-pressure assignment that is like an MBA on steroids.

Because of all these demands, command is optional and Officers compete for command spots. Command is considered an honor and is a strong discriminator for promotion boards. Brigade/battalion commanders normally start looking for company commander replacements six months out. You won't receive an official announcement in the mail but it's likely that your husband will have some idea that he is being considered. You will probably find out that he has been selected two to three months before he assumes command. The company commander will be in the same career field as his or her Soldiers. For example, if your husband is an MP, he will command a military police company. Often, Second Lieutenants are moved up within their company to take command when the commander rotates out. But this isn't always the case. Certainly, the top brass try and match a Soldier's personality and leadership style with the right unit, but it is really more about the rotation cycle and where a particular Soldier is needed. There are a lot of moving parts to manage and there isn't an exact science as far as when, exactly, your husband will take command. And, unfortunately, "lives close to the armory" isn't one of the things that the National Guard looks at when matching up commanders with companies. Your husband could be assigned to a company that is an hour or two from your home. But that's just how the Guard works; consider it an adventure!

The Change-of-Command Ceremony

Your official participation in your husband's command begins with the change-of-command ceremony. Change-of-command ceremonies are held in all branches of the military, at all levels. This traditional ceremony is a legal and symbolic passing of authority and responsibility from one command to the next. During the ceremony, you will be formally introduced to the company and battalion leadership. Official orders are read and the unit flag (officially called a guidon) is passed from the outgoing command to the incoming commander. The senior NCO also participates in the passing of the colors. The purpose of the ceremony portion of the program is to honor the outgoing commander and his family members. This is THEIR day to be formally recognized for the extra time and effort that they have dedicated to the company. It gives them a chance to say goodbye to the Soldiers in the company and (hopefully) recognize the long-serving members of the company in front of the "Big Brass" that typically attend such ceremonies.

The change-of-command ceremony will be held over a regular drill weekend in the armory or company HQ. It is the outgoing commander's responsibility to schedule and plan the change-of-command ceremony.

However, in practice, both outgoing and incoming commanders will work with their traditional and full-time staffs to make it happen. The NCOs at the unit take great pride in how this special ceremony is conducted at their unit. They are experts in this arena and will hold company rehearsals to make sure that everybody knows what to do and when to do it. They will escort you to your seat and take care of everything. If you are the outgoing commander's wife, enjoy yourself because you don't have to worry about a thing. If you are the incoming commander's wife, the only thing you have to worry about is planning the reception portion of the program.

Your To-Do List

If there's one thing I've learned during my tenure as a Guard wife, it's to be proactive. My husband operates on a need-to-know-basis. I operate on a want-to-know basis. Yes, I need to know the date of an event but I also want to know exactly what I am in for. The good news is that during your husband's command, there will only be a few key events that you're going to have to be there for. The bad news is that you won't be receiving a "Spouse's Introduction to Company Command" packet in the mail.

There usually aren't formal, mailed invitations to a change of command but the dates are determined well in advance so be sure to mark your calendar. Dates can slide due to unforeseen circumstances and scheduling conflicts. Make sure to check in with your husband every couple of weeks to make sure plans haven't changed. Unless there is an emergency or longstanding engagement that you can't get out of, you really should attend the change-of-command ceremony. This is a big day for your Soldier and you won't want to miss it.

The Reception

It is the incoming commander's responsibility to plan the reception portion of the program. There will be resources in the company to help you make the arrangements. In the regular Army, the outgoing commander does not attend the reception portion of the program (unless the new commander asks him to). In the Guard, however, there are so few opportunities to get together that the outgoing commander usually stays for the reception. This is his choice and either way is appropriate. Just as the ceremony is about the outgoing commander, the reception is about the incoming commander. The reception is a time for the new commander to meet and greet everybody. It is also a time for him to introduce his wife and children to the unit and battalion leadership.

As far as planning goes, this is a casual social gathering and you shouldn't worry about it too much. Consult your husband a few weeks before the ceremony to find out what he has in mind. You will pay for this out of your own pocket, so budget accordingly ($200 is a minimum number to plan around—many spend more. Don't be afraid of over-budgeting. You will be remembered very fondly at the next day's chow if there are leftovers). Keep it simple but thoughtful. The reception is typically held on-site and all of the Soldiers will attend (however, their family members won't) so make sure to get a headcount in advance so you will be prepared. Of the 150 person company, you can expect 100 to be present at the ceremony. However, you can also expect representatives from your higher commands as well as peers from other units to drop by. This means, you may be serving up to 200 people.

Remember, you aren't providing a meal for the Soldiers (the Army does this on drill weekends) but you will provide beverages and light fare. Here is a basic shopping list:

- Non-alcoholic refreshments—bottled water, soda, iced tea, or juice. (I like to make punch because it can be served at any time of day, is very festive, and goes a long way! If you don't own a big punch bowl—and there isn't one available through the unit—rent one at a party supply store.) Don't forget the ice!
- For a morning reception: light breakfast fare such as mini muffins, bagels, quick breads, mini quiches, and fruit.
- For a late afternoon reception (after "chow"): chips, vegetable trays, cheese and crackers, or my favorite: a dessert buffet.
- No matter what time . . . provide a full sheet cake. You can have the unit's name written on the cake or use the unit colors or crest if you would like. Don't include the outgoing or incoming commander's names on the cake.
- Paper goods—napkins, cups, plates, plastic utensils, plastic serving bowls for chips, cake knife, and plastic tablecloths. Be sure to bring any serving utensils required! The armory will not have these.
- Flowers and decorations are optional but add a nice touch. I also like to bring in all of my own platters, bowls, vases, and serving pieces.

The morning of the ceremony, or the day before if you can swing it, find a space in the armory where you can set up for the reception. The HQ staff and mess staff will assist you with logistics (for future reference, get in good with the mess staff because they are the ones with the cookies). If there is a separate side room available, that is ideal. If not, the food and beverages can be set up in the same room as the ceremony. You don't need to worry about setting up tables or moving chairs around. Just make sure you have checked the items on your grocery list and your husband and his team will take care of the rest. Feel free to put your own stamp on things. If you want to make your famous artichoke dip, do it! If you want to bring in your own linens and serving pieces, go for it. If you want to have background music, that's great. Just know that these receptions are more about socializing and meeting new people than having a great dining experience. Don't break the bank or get tripped up in details. People are more interested in meeting you than fancy floral arrangements.

For a recent change of command ceremony, I was really stuck on what to do. The ceremony was held right before lunch which meant that serving the usual munchies wouldn't work. We opted for a dessert buffet. After the ceremony, we made an announcement that we would host a dessert reception after lunch. We ate with the Soldiers and hosted the ceremony directly afterwards. A trip to Costco provided everything we needed: cookie platters, mini brownies, and bulk candies. We served a sheet cake and also served ice cream. I manned the punch bowl and Jon scooped ice cream. It was a big hit.

Other Ways to Help

Offer to review your husband's bio. The people coordinating the ceremony will put together a program that includes an agenda as well as information about the powers that be. Detailed bios of the incoming and outgoing commanders are included in the program and your husband will be asked to provide his information in a timely manner. His bio will include detailed information about his military career and achievements. The last paragraph includes information about his civilian career, volunteer activities, the name of your hometown, and the names of immediate family members (spouse, children, and parents). A simple line such as: "CPT Doe married the former Anne Smith in 1999. The couple lives in city, state where he is involved in American Legion Post xxx. The Does have two children: Jane, 7 and Robert, 4" will do the trick. At the end of the bio, it is perfectly appropriate to include a short tribute to relatives who have served in the military such as, "His grandfather served with the Marines in World War II where he was a survivor of the attack on Pearl Harbor," or "His eldest brother, Jim, is a Vietnam veteran." Make sure to save your copy of the program as it is a wonderful keepsake.

If you live far from the armory, consider staying in a hotel the night before the change-of-command ceremony. Some states offer a program that provides free hotel lodging on drill weekends for Soldiers who live 50 miles or more from the armory. Ask your husband to find out if you are eligible for this, and, if you are, ask him to make the arrangements. But even if you are not eligible, the cost for a typical hotel is minimal compared to the hassle of driving back and forth. Be warned, however, that your husband will be busy at drill and will NOT be able to spend much time with you. Use the time to explore the area.

A few weeks before the change-of-command ceremony, ask for the names of the following key players AND their spouses: outgoing commander, former commanders, NCOs, Junior Officers, and Battalion Commander. Look over their names and try and get your head around who is who. At the ceremony, ask your husband to introduce you to these key players. If he is busy, introduce yourself. Just remember, the higher the rank, the longer the line is to meet them. Just do what feels natural. Remind your husband to plan some brief remarks for the ceremony. He doesn't need to give a long, formal speech but he should definitely prepare his talking points in advance. He should contact some people in the unit before the ceremony and collect some positive information about the outgoing commander. Decide what you are wearing and what your kids are wearing well in advance. The Soldiers will be in their ACUs. This isn't a formal affair, which to me means no sequins and no hosiery but you definitely want to wear something nice (no jeans, shorts, or flip flops). Wear what you would wear out to a nice restaurant for lunch. In the summer months, a nice sundress or skirt is perfect. If you want to play it safe, my preferred method, invest in a nice pair of black dress pants and wear them with a simple blouse or sweater set. If you have children and you love to doll them up, now is the time! Knock yourself out and dress your daughter in a smocked dress with patent leather buckle shoes. Horrify your husband by dressing your little boy in short pants. It is perfectly appropriate to dress your kids, including teenagers, in a nice, Sunday style outfit. However, any clean outfit will do. The point is that this is a special day for your family and you should all look your best. Make sure you take some pictures because you will want these later. It is fine to invite a few of your close family members to the event (your parents, your spouse's parents) but is best to keep your personal invitation list to a minimum. You can invite a few more people when your husband is the outgoing commander.

Children in Command

You will be seated in the front row during the change of command ceremony. If you have small children, you may want to have a second set of hands to manage the children if they get antsy. You may be the only person with children at the event. Most kids love being in the armory but that doesn't mean that they have the run of the place. Kids have very short attention spans so pack some things for them to do and keep an eye on them. Anybody with small children knows that you can never really enjoy yourself when you are out in public. This is your husband's event and he will help you the best that he can but it may not be possible. Try not to shoot him too many dirty looks when you are stuck in a corner with the kids (you can get even with him at home later). One of the best parts about being married to the company commander is that, more often than not, some of those good-natured Privates may offer you a hand with the kids. If they do, hand them off for a few minutes and make a run for it. Use the opportunity to mingle with your husband's new co-workers.

Settling In

Your husband will be given his own office area—an office that has belonged to the commander since the armory was built. Remember this when your HGTV sensibilities kick in. There is no need to redecorate. Oddly enough, Army people don't notice that their curtains are forty years old or that the vinyl couch is uncomfortable. If you have small children, you can keep some toys and art supplies in his office for visits. But give the outgoing commander a chance to move his things out before you move in to his office or take over his parking spot.

Don't remove anything in the office no matter how useless or disgusting it looks. Many of the things in a commander's office are there for nostalgic reasons. I found this out when I asked that a stuffed snake be removed from my husband's new office. Let's just say that it didn't happen. We've long since moved on, but that nasty old snake is s-s-s-s-still there.

Every armory has an NCOs room and an Officer's Room for Lieutenants. When there is a function, the spouses of those Soldiers can use these rooms to hang out. Events don't always start on time and it is nice to have a place where you can relax and kill time. This arrangement comes in very handy if you have small children. If your Soldier is an NCO or Officer and you have access to these rooms, it is important to know that you are a guest. The rooms are meant for the Soldiers to work in and are only on loan. If you see another family member who needs a place to give a baby a bottle or stash a stroller, do the right thing and show them to the Officer's rooms. It doesn't matter if they are married to a Private. Common courtesy always comes before rank.

Family Programs

In addition to making sure the company is mission-ready, the commander is responsible for all of the programs and activities within the company. The most important outreach to families is through the Family Readiness Group (FRG). It is the commander's job to make sure that the company has a chartered and proficient family readiness FRG in place (we will go into much more detail about FRGs in Chapter Nine).

Some commanders get lucky and already have a great FRG leader in place. Others may have to recruit the right person for this important position. The FRG leader needs to have a good personality, confident demeanor, leadership ability, knowledge of the organization and how it runs, and enough time to commit to this important job. Most importantly, the FRG leader must have the "commander's ear."

The commander's ear is something that you can help with. Your husband is going to be extremely busy during his command and he probably won't be able to manage unit business during his civilian work day. That means that much of his work will be done in the evenings. Make sure you know what your FRG leader's family situation is. If she has small children, she will have times of the day when she focuses on her FRG responsibilities. Make sure she knows that she can call you if she needs to get in touch with your husband. Always push her messages through quickly and make sure he gets back to her as soon as possible. You may be able to provide her some of the answers that she needs based on your familiarity with your husband's schedule and preferences. If the unit is fortunate enough to have a great FRG leader in place, count your blessings and don't rock the boat! If you don't have an FRG leader in place, and a good candidate doesn't step forward, you will lead the FRG. Do the best you can with the resources available to you.

One of your husband's first orders of business is to introduce you to the FRG leader. Remember, this person is volunteering countless hours to help your husband. To get things off to the right start, make sure that the FRG leader is invited to the change-of-command ceremony. If she is unable to attend, find a time to meet with her for lunch (and pick up the tab). Even if you have to take a day off work to meet her at her convenience, it is well worth the time and effort because she is taking on an enormous responsibility and a successful FRG reflects well on the unit. Get her contact information and find out her preferred method of communication i.e., e-mail or phone. Let her know that she can contact you anytime she needs something, especially if that something is the commander's ear.

Throughout your husband's command, make sure he communicates with the FRG leader and recognizes her at all company events. If the unit deploys, you will work closely with the FRG leader. The best role you can play is to support the FRG organization's effort to communicate and assist family members. Make sure that she has your current contact information and be prepared to help field phone calls from family members. Show up at events and make sure that everybody knows how to reach you. During deployments, FRG leaders receive phone calls at all hours of the day or night from family members dealing with all sorts of difficulties. Make sure that you are available to help the FRG leader with these situations.

Stay in close contact with the FRG leader and other volunteers. It is likely that formal meetings will be held at the armory. Do your best to attend meetings. If you live too far from the armory to attend meetings, make sure to schedule weekly calls with the FRG leader and find out how you can be of assistance. With all the technology available today, we don't have to meet face-to-face to keep in touch and support each other.

Just remember that the FRG leader has a lot on her plate during a deployment (if you are the FRG leader, you already know this). She has a lot of people who need her time and assistance. You need to be a rock for her and give her the back up that she needs. If your husband is overseas, remind him to e-mail the FRG leader and thank her for her ongoing efforts. He should also go out of his way to sing her praises to all the Soldiers in the company.

Planning Events/Programs

In most units, the full-time NCO staffers do a great job planning and hosting events for family members. Many units have a family event in the summer and one around the holidays. These are run like a well-oiled machine, and sometimes, you need only show up. If you want to help, soliciting donations for door prizes or drawings is a great place to start. Since you probably live in a different community than where the armory is, you have an untapped resource. In other units, the social calendar is more up for grabs and you are welcome to offer ideas for social activities within the company. The key players who determine company programs and activities are 1) the commander 2) the First Sergeant and 3) the FRG leader. Every company has funds available to spend on events that build morale. The rules about how money is raised and allocated are very strict and must be followed exactly. When there is a change of command, an audit is conducted. After this is completed, the incoming commander is added to accounts and has signature authority over all expenditures. Additionally, other military personnel within the unit may be given signature authority. You, however, don't have authority over any of the unit's monies. But that doesn't mean you can't make some suggestions. Just make sure that you take some time to anticipate what the costs will be and propose a budget.

Don't be surprised if some of your new and creative ideas are greeted with skepticism by the administrative NCO at the company. But don't take it personally. Most companies have a way of doing things that work for them. When people hear new ideas, they think "uh oh, sounds like more work for me." The best way to try something new is to sell it to the full-timers and the prominent, long-time members of the company. If they are enthusiastic, they will spread that enthusiasm to the rest of the company. If they are skeptical —you will fight an uphill battle. Just remember that they are the ones who have their finger on the pulse. The NCOs are in close contact with the troops and know what types of events will be well-received. And remember, if you are lucky enough to get the stamp of approval for a new idea, it's up to you to make it happen.

Reaching Out

Many of the wives in the company have been involved in the Guard—and in the company—for years. Utilize any opportunity that you have to get their guidance and advice. Your husband may be the commander, but you are new to the job. Get help from the wives who know the lay of the land. Make sure you get to know the First Sergeant's wife and always treat her with respect and kindness. As the senior Noncommissioned Officer in the company, her husband is the single biggest center of gravity in the unit of which you have just become a member.

A great way to reach out to your husband's new co-workers is by hosting a gathering at your home. If you love to entertain and want to get to know your Guard family better, invite people to your home. During your husband's command, you will meet a new circle of interesting people and you should take the opportunity to get to know them better. In the Guard, we are all so spread around and everybody is busy. Initially, I thought that people would be put off by an invitation to a dinner party, but I was pleasantly surprised to find out that most welcomed it. During your husband's command, here are some of the people who you may want to extend an invitation to:

- The First Sergeant and spouse
- Company Officers, NCOs, and spouses
- Battalion Commander and spouse
- Other company commanders in the battalion

You don't have to have a big house or fancy furniture to throw a nice party. Entertain in a way that fits your style and budget. We live in a very modest home and our kids have ruined every piece of furniture that we own. I make up for that by entertaining at night. Candlelight is very forgiving and can hide everything from a stain on the sofa to dust bunnies in the corner.

If you decide to have an event at your home, check with your husband to see if there are any conflicting Guard events, but don't waste time trying to figure out what works for everybody's schedule. Pick a date that works for you, make your guest list, send invitations in the mail (I'm not a fan of Evites for intimate parties), and see what happens. Set a firm RSVP deadline and give people the option of sending their RSVP via e-mail. If people can make it work with their schedules, they will. Don't pressure people to attend or take it personally if they can't attend. If people fail to RSVP, don't read into it. They may have misplaced the invitation or just forgotten about it. If you are having a formal, sit-down dinner and need an absolute headcount, follow up with a quick phone call or e-mail. But if your party is casual or buffet-style, assume they won't be attending and be pleasantly surprised if they do show up. Even if your big dinner party turns into a quiet dinner with one other couple, it is a chance to get to know each other better. Sometimes those are the best parties of all.

The Rumor Mill

I wish I could say that the Guard is a gossip-free organization but, it's not. Just like every workplace (and family, for that matter), the Guard boasts quite an active rumor mill. And, very few people can say that they haven't been a part of it at one time or another. It's hard to believe that as busy as we all are, and as honorable as the organization is, we still have the time to gossip about each other. I also think it is sad that rumors run especially rampant during deployments because that is when we need each other's loyalty and support the most.

Some of the rumors are just part of being in the Guard. After 9/11, my husband was a Lieutenant. I was new to the Guard and didn't know anything about deployments. I was constantly on the horn with my informants trying to figure out when and if our Soldiers would be deployed. After they were deployed, even though I didn't have the time to attend any FRG meetings, I somehow found the time to get the dirt on what went down at the meetings. I'm not proud of my behavior but I was new to the organization and just didn't understand that harmless chit chat can quickly turn into feeding the rumor mill. Guilty as charged.

As the commander's wife, it is just as much your job as his to control OPSEC (Operational Security). You may be privy to information that your husband has confided in you about personnel decisions, possible deployments, and other matters, but that information is confidential. Any reconnaissance that you gather is Army business and not public information. Any e-mails that you see flying through your home PC are for your husband's eyes only and if you happen to see them, just pretend that you didn't. Don't EVER repeat any information that has been confided in you by your husband or his superiors. And don't EVER speculate about official

Army business. This includes possible deployment dates/redeployment dates/extensions.

The longer that you are in the Guard family, the more people you will meet. People will get comfortable with you and will talk about what's going on in the organization. We all want to know who is moving where and who is doing what. That's human nature. But there is a fine line from stating a fact such as "x got a divorce," or "x is leaving the Guard," and going into all the nitty-gritty details of a personal or professional event—especially when you haven't witnessed such an event with your own eyes.

Here's the thing about gossip . . . on some level, we all like to be in the know. The best people will let things go in one ear and out the other and write it off as harmless talk. Others will repeat what they hear. And it all just seems like sport. Until, that is, the nasty rumor is about YOU. When you are the object of gossip, you will realize how hurtful it can be. The first time my husband came home and told me about what the rumor mill was saying about us, I was stunned. We tried to figure out who would say such things and what the motivation could be. But after I thought about it, I was able to put it in perspective because I believe the following:

- People who spread vicious rumors usually have some issues in their own lives. They may be insecure or jealous. They deserve your pity, not your anger.
- The higher up a Soldier gets in the organization and the more support he or she has from his superiors, the more he or she will be plagued with gossip. It's lonely at the top.

As the wife of a company commander, you will hear a lot of rumors. You may even hear some about yourself! Don't ever bite. Just say something like:

- "You know I don't care what people say about me. So anyways . . . how is your Christmas shopping going?"
- "People must be really bored if they're talking about me. So, did you finish that project at work?"
- "Hmmm, I hadn't heard that. Anyways, how are your kids doing in school?"
- "Sounds like just another dumb rumor. So, what have you been up to? (Besides spreading around evil gossip, that is.)"

- "Oh please. I get my gossip fix from "US Weekly." Speaking of which, did you hear the latest?"

QUICK TIPS FOR AVOIDING GOSSIP

- Know who is in your corner. Be loyal to your Guard friends and don't sell them out just to fit in.
- Understand that jealousy is the motivation behind most gossip.
- Remind your husband that, as company commander, people are watching his actions. He needs to act appropriately, especially where female Soldiers are concerned.
- Spend your time with other Guard couples who have solid marriages and whose number one priority is their family.
- Always be professional and kind to everybody, but politely distance yourself from people who don't share your values.
- Don't try and defend people or dig for details or sources. If you do, that will become part of the story and help fuel the fire. Just make it go away through your disinterest. Then, change the subject.
- If you need to vent or get something off your chest, do it with somebody who isn't associated with the Guard (sister, mother, or friend).
- If you do confide in a Guard friend, be absolutely sure that you can trust them and count on their discretion.

What Really Matters

Even if you don't have a lot of free time to give to the Guard during your husband's command, the best thing that you can do is support him unconditionally. Being in the military is a calling, in a way. It isn't just a regular job. It is just too important. During his command, he will have to work very hard. The hours are long. Just remember that he's not the only one working overtime. You aren't the only wife who feels a little neglected from time-to-time. We always hear that families come first, and we do in our Soldier's hearts. But the demands of command mean that many times, his job will take time away from you and your family. This isn't because he doesn't want to be with you or is choosing work over you or your kids, it's because duty calls.

Being a company commander is demanding. And being married to a company commander is demanding, too. Sometimes it's hard not to take things personally. We think that our Soldiers have a choice in the hours they work, or the homework they are expected to complete between drills. Before your husband's command, drill seems like something Soldiers just show up for. But during your husband's command, you will see what it takes to keep a company running smoothly. The welfare of the Soldiers and their families is foremost in your spouse's mind. Everybody has to pull their weight. Your unwavering support and encouragement is the key to your Soldier's success.

Wrap Up:

- Your tenure begins at the change-of-command ceremony. Be prepared for the ceremony and enjoy it. You are responsible for the reception portion of the program, but this is a casual affair and shouldn't take much planning.
- You don't have to be the FRG leader, but there has to be one. If you are lucky enough to have a good FRG leader in place, count your blessings! Be a resource for her and offer your ongoing assistance. If there isn't an FRG leader in place and a volunteer doesn't step forward, as the commander's wife, by default, it will be you. Accept the position and do the best that you can.
- Put your own stamp on things and make your own traditions. Command is an opportunity to make new friends and solidify your place in the Guard Family. Enjoy this once-in-a-lifetime experience. If you want to celebrate a mission accomplished or give your fellow spouses a morale boost when they need it the most, be proactive and plan something yourself.
- You are the official rumor patrol. When Soldiers are deployed, rumors fly. It is your job to squelch rumors, not fuel them.

Chapter 7

The Benefits of
Being a Guardsman

It is an honor to be married to a member of the Armed Services and if we ever forget, our fellow Americans remind us with smiles, handshakes, and a sincere thank you. They know that military families make a lot of personal sacrifices to serve a greater good and in our hearts, we know it too. But let's be honest, sometimes the Guard can be a real inconvenience. Drill weekends seem to pop up out of nowhere. When our Soldiers are away attending a two-week course out of town, we forget about the work they have to do during the day (and the homework at night) and hone in on a dinner or two out-on-the-towns with their fellow Soldiers. During long-term deployments, it is especially hard to see the upside of Guard life. We all have these feelings and it is natural to feel frustrated from time-to-time. Let me share something with you that helps when you feel like Guard life isn't a cakewalk: focus on the tangible benefits of Guard membership.

The mission of this book is to provide you with a high-level view of the nuts and bolts of National Guard life and delve into detail in areas that have not been explored before. As far as military benefits are concerned, there are hundreds of websites and publications that detail them all. Rather than re-invent the wheel, this chapter will focus on connecting Soldiers and family members to benefits and providing information on some key Guard benefits.

First Things First: Connecting to Benefits

Before we discuss the key benefits, you need to know that if your Soldier isn't in the system, you will not receive any benefits. The Army, like all large businesses, sports its fair share of bureaucracy. And bureaucracy means paperwork. We all know about paperwork. Even after you shuck all the junk mail every day, you are left with a hearty stack of paperwork that needs attention. Whether we are registering children for school or completing forms for our bank, accountant, or employer, the squeaky wheel gets the grease and we usually prioritize things based on the nag factor. If somebody keeps reminding you to get something done, you will do it simply to get them to stop bugging you about it.

When it comes to Guard paperwork, nobody is going to nag you about it. It is up to your Soldier to get this done without prompting. I used to think there was a Big Brother looking out for me when it came to the National Guard. Some all-knowing Sergeant Major with little white wings fluttering over my shoulder, tracking my every move and reporting it back to the Army. "Uh, Ma'am? Your husband's ex-girlfriend from 1996 is listed as his beneficiary . . . let's get that taken care of today," or "You just moved and didn't tell the Army? Tsk. Tsk. We need to get that changed right away." But after experiencing a few misunderstandings, I came to understand that the responsibility lies with the Soldier.

Your Soldier is the only person with the authority to make things happen as far as records are concerned and anything that the Army asks for, the Army needs. Our Soldiers are involved in a dangerous and unpredictable profession. The Army must know how to reach you during drills, annual training, mobilizations, and deployments. Sometimes the business at hand is simple and straight forward. Sometimes there is an emergency. Whatever the situation, time is of the essence and the Army will look to the information that your Soldier provided to get in touch with you ASAP. As far as benefits are concerned, Soldier records must be accurate to connect you to the benefits that you are entitled.

DEERS (Not the Kind with Antlers)

Soldiers provide vital personal information at the unit level and the unit manages and updates all applicable systems, including the Defense Enrollment Eligibility Reporting System (DEERS) and the Defense

Integrated Military Resources System (DIMHRS). DEERS is the acronym that you will hear often and for good reason. DEERS is the backbone of the military system and lists Soldiers and dependants eligible for military pay and benefits. Soldiers are properly vetted before being entered into DEERS and if a Soldier isn't in DEERS, the military does not know they exist. Mistakes in DEERS can cause problems with pay and benefits.

Many Guard units prompt Soldiers to update their records during their birthday month. Other units take care of everything at once and update all Soldier records during a dedicated month such as December. And you guessed it—it is no accident that this often coincides with a family day event. The standard information collected or reviewed includes:

- Next of Kin (NOK) data on a Record of Emergency Data (contact information for a Soldier's spouse, children, parents, and any other people who should be notified if the Soldier becomes a casualty).
- Beneficiary information for Servicemembers' Group Life Insurance (SGLI) and additional/private insurance policies.
- Retirement Point Accounting System (RPAS) data.

Outside of official unit paperwork pushes, when a Soldier has a life event (marriage, divorce, remarriage, birth or adoption of a child, change of civilian employer, move) it is up to them to approach the readiness NCO at their unit and fill out the appropriate paperwork to update DEERS. Feel free to remind them early and often.

If Soldiers are being deployed, there are different processes in place and additional information required. They may be asked to provide additional information during SRP (Soldier Readiness Processing) such as family readiness/ESGR (Employer Support of Guard and Reserve) paperwork. Vital information is sent to family program resources and serves as a trigger to make sure that your family is in the system and that you receive all the benefits of a full-time, active duty military family.

CAC: Your All-Access Pass

In addition to being in the system, members of the active duty Armed Forces, Selected Reserves, National Guard, and other government employees are issued a Common Access Card (CAC). This is a special, government-issued photo identification card that contains an integrated circuit chip with two digital fingerprints, digital photo, organizational affiliation, and other information about your Soldier. The CAC's barcode includes their Social Security Number, benefit information, pay grade, and other confidential data. The CAC is used to enter federal buildings and controlled spaces (such as military bases), log on securely to DoD networks, systems, and websites, encrypt e-mail, and electronically sign documents. All eligible personnel must be entered into DEERS and meet all Real-Time Automated Personnel Identification System (RAPIDS) requirements. Cards are color-coded to identify specific affiliations and the type/color of card issued depends on many factors including duty status. The CAC is the Soldier's passport to the military world and they need it to do their job.

If a Soldier is home (not on active duty in excess of 30 days) their spouse is eligible to receive a CAC privilege card (DD Form 1173-1). This card is used to tap into both private sector military perks (such as discounted movie tickets) and official military privileges (such as Military Welfare and Recreation facilities and shopping at military commissaries or exchanges). To obtain a new card or update an expired card, go to www.cac.mil and link to the RAPIDS center site to find a list of locations closest to your zip code. RAPIDS centers are located on military installations and there may be one at your battalion or headquarters building. Make sure you bring the required documentation listed on the website and call in advance to find out how processing works. Some locations set up appointments in advance while others are first come, first served. Some offices are only open certain days of the week. Others are closed over the lunch hour. Some close early on certain days. Some locations that you would assume are Guard only because they are located at Guard state or battalion headquarters buildings, actually service active duty military installations as well. If this is the case, you could be waiting for hours to get your identification (or update an expired ID card). CALL BEFORE YOU GO!

If your Soldier is deployed or is on active duty for more than 30 days, you will be issued a different kind of CAC (DD Form 1173) during Soldier Readiness Processing. This ID is equal to that of an active duty military spouse and serves as your insurance card if you receive medical benefits through the Army. Other military family members (i.e., children, former spouses) may also be eligible to receive a military ID. Lost CACs must be reported immediately through a Soldier's chain of command or at a RAPIDS center so that a replacement can be issued.

Guard Compensation Package

Now let's talk about the fun things, the perks of Guard life. From a regular paycheck to a retirement pension, Guard life certainly has its perks; too many to list in a single book chapter. In addition to the benefits offered through the military and the Veteran's Administration, there is a lot of assistance available to Guard families through private channels as well as each individual state. The challenge is getting your arms around all of the resources.

In the spirit of providing the information you need without overloading you with details that you can find in other places, I will focus on the following key benefits:

- Pay
- Retirement Pension
- Health and Dental Insurance
- Life Insurance
- Survivor Benefits
- Thrift Savings Plan (TSP)
- Bonuses
- Money for Education
- Space-A Travel
- Commissary, Exchange and Morale, Welfare, and Recreation (MWR)

In addition to the benefits listed above, Guardsmen activated for more than 30 days receive the same entitlements as active duty Soldiers. This means that many of the key benefits listed above (such as health insurance and Space-A travel) are enhanced or expanded to include family members.

Pay

Everybody knows that our Soldiers don't join the Army to receive a paycheck, but certainly your Soldier's paycheck tops the list of tangible benefits. How your Soldier is paid, the amount of payment, and the benefits he or she receives depend on their duty status. The military compensation system has more than separate types of pay and allowances. Soldiers can access all pay information by logging into https://mypay.dfas.mil.

Regardless of your Soldier's duty status, their basic pay is based on their current pay grade. Pay grade is determined by rank and years in service. Marital status, number of dependents, and place of residence don't affect a Guardsman's basic pay. Pay and allowances are established by law and pay tables are available online and break pay down in many ways (Officers, enlisted, one drill period/one UTA, one drill weekend/4 MUTAs, 15-day Annual Training, etc.). To find your Soldier's pay, you will need to know their pay grade and years of Guard service. Basic pay is taxable income unless your Soldier has Combat Zone exclusion. A Soldier doing traditional Guard duty (weekend drills, AT) will be paid once a month and receive their checks via automatic deposit. Mobilized Soldiers are paid twice a month based on actual days worked. Your Soldier's paycheck will increase with their rank and years in service and military personnel typically receive an annual pay raise of 2-4% which goes into effect every January.

Retirement/Military Pension

Back in the good old days, companies offered pensions. Employees gave the company 20 to 30 years and their employer gave them a pension check every month for the rest of their lives. Those days are long gone. Very few companies offer pensions. But the Army does offer a pension system and, in my opinion, this is one of the most important perks of Guard service. Once you know how the system works, I know you will share my excitement.

The Guard retirement system is extremely complicated and there are caveats and exceptions to all of the rules. The information I am presenting represents the top level plan that applies to most Guard members. Keep in mind that every Soldier's situation is different and eligibility, date that retirement pay starts, and the amount of pay received depends on many factors. The best written explanation of the retirement system is found on the website www.armyg1.army.mil where you will find useful calculators and tools to help you determine retirement benefits.

Both Army personnel and Guard Soldiers must put in 20 years before they collect their pension. The big difference is that in the regular armed services, military personnel collect their pension right away, even if they are only 40 years old when their 20 years are up. Once they have put in their 20 and retire, they get their check every month. In the Reserve forces, military personnel don't see a dime until they are 60 years old (there are a few exceptions to this, but not many). In the military, retirement benefits are connected to the service member's DIEMS (Date Initially Entered Military Service). If your Soldier joined the military on June 1st, they will earn one retirement year on June 1st of the following year and every year after that. If your Soldier was in the Army before joining the Guard, their DIEMS will be based on when they started their career in the military, not when they signed on with the Guard. Your Soldier's start date will never change, even if they take a break in service.

The ins and outs of the Guard retirement plans are complicated but, if you have a question, there is an office in the state headquarters devoted to assisting Soldiers in figuring out how the retirement plan affects them. Inquiries should be made through your Soldier's chain of command.

Health and Dental Insurance

TRICARE is the health care program serving the military community. TRICARE supplements military health care resources (i.e., military treatment facilities located on military bases) with networks of civilian health care professionals, institutions, and pharmacies. To be eligible for TRICARE benefits, Soldiers and family members must be registered in DEERS. TRICARE offers several health plan options to meet the needs of Soldiers and their families.

Traditional Guardsmen Benefits

Soldiers on military duty for 30 days or less (i.e., weekend drills, AT, other short periods of active duty, etc.) are automatically covered under Line of Duty Care for any injury, illness, or disease that occurred or was aggravated in the line of duty. This includes injuries sustained when traveling directly to or from the place of duty. In addition, members of the Guard and their family members are eligible for different medical/dental benefits depending on their duty status. TRICARE Reserve Select (TRS) is a premium-based health plan that qualified National Guard members who are not on active duty orders may purchase. To qualify, Soldiers need to log into the secure Guard and Reserve Web Portal (they can get current information through their chain of command). They will be required to print and sign the

TRS Request Form (DD Form 2896-1) and mail or fax the completed TRS Request Form along with the first month's premium payment to the regional contractor listed on the web portal.

The monthly premium amount is based on the type of coverage selected (TRS Member-Only or TRS Member and Family). The first premium can be paid by check, money order, or cashier's check (payable to the regional contractor) or by Visa®/MasterCard®. Regular monthly premiums may be paid via Electronic Fund Transfer (EFT)/automatic bank withdrawal, automatic credit/debit card withdrawal, or direct billing. Coverage begins on the first day of the first or second month (whichever option is selected on the TRS Request Form) following the postmark of the TRS Request Form. For example, if the form is postmarked in May, the Soldier chooses for coverage to begin on the first day of the next month, June, or on the first day of the second month, July. After the initial premium payment, the regional contractor will bill the Soldier by the 10th of each month. Payments are due no later than the 30th of each month and payments are applied to the following month of coverage. Failure to pay premiums by the date due will result in termination of coverage effective the last day of the month last paid and a one-year purchase lockout. Premium amounts may be adjusted annually, on a calendar-year basis, in accordance with applicable legislation.

Once qualified, plans may be purchased at any time throughout the year. The type of TRS coverage, TRS Member-Only or TRS Member and Family, can be changed after a qualifying life event:

- Marriage
- Birth or adoption
- Placement of child in the legal custody of the member by order of the court
- Divorce or annulment
- Death of a spouse or family member
- Family member loses eligibility (e.g., child turns 21 or 23 if enrolled in college)

Soldiers must report the life event to a military personnel office and record the information in DEERS. After DEERS is updated, the type of TRS coverage can be changed. To change the TRS coverage, download a new TRS Request Form from the Guard and Reserve Web Portal, complete the form, and submit it to your regional contractor postmarked within 60 days of the qualifying life event. The change in coverage is effective the date the qualifying life event occurred. Changes to TRS coverage that don't involve a change in family composition (e.g., eligibility for other health coverage) can be made at any time.

Guard members who are issued delayed-effective-date active duty orders for more than 30 days in support of a contingency operation, may qualify for early eligibility for TRICARE medical and dental benefits. Additionally, when Guard members qualify for pre-activation benefits, family members who are registered in DEERS are also covered under TRICARE up to 90 days before the sponsor's active duty service begins. The member's personnel office will tell members if they are eligible for pre-activation benefits when they receive their delayed effective-date active duty orders. If you don't meet these early eligibility requirements, your and your family'coverage will begin on the first day of your orders.

Active Duty Benefits

Soldiers on active duty for more than 30 consecutive days (and their family members) are eligible for comprehensive health care coverage under several TRICARE options. The type of plan depends on where they live when activated. In most cases, the Soldier will receive his or her medical care at the nearest Military Treatment Facility (MTF). Family members also receive medical care from an MTF (if there is one close to them) or from civilian doctors and dentists in their own communities who are in the military physician/dental provider network.

Dental Coverage

TRICARE medical and dental are two different programs and you must enroll in each separately. The TRICARE Dental Program (TDP) is open to all Guardsmen and their dependents. Families pay the premium and there is no government participation. Soldiers can enroll their family at any time and must make a 12-month commitment. They must fill out the enrollment form and provide the first month's premium by the 20th of the month. Coverage will begin the first of the following month. TDP works exactly the same as dental plans offered through civilian employers. You are issued and mailed an ID card and encouraged to go to dentists in the network who will process your insurance paperwork. The plan covers 100% of the costs of routine preventative care (such as cleanings) and portions of more involved procedures. The rest comes out of your pocket. For more information on coverage and a list of network providers, visit www.Tricare DentalProgram.com.

When Soldiers are activated for 31 days or more, they are automatically disenrolled from the TDP and covered by active duty dental benefits. In this case, they will receive dental care at MTF. Their family's dental care needs will continue to be covered under the TRICARE Dental Program if they are enrolled, with no break in coverage. Soldiers are automatically re-enrolled in the TDP upon deactivation and their coverage automatically resumes.

Life Insurance

Servicemembers' Group Life insurance (SGLI) is a Veteran's Administration (VA) program that provides low cost group life insurance to members of the Armed Forces. Members are automatically insured for the maximum amount of $400,000. SGLI coverage includes Traumatic Injury Protection ranging from $25,000 to $100,000 depending on the nature of the injury. The cost for a Guardsman is $28 per year for $400,000 of coverage. Title 10 Soldiers pay $27 per month for the maximum of $400,000. SGLI coverage, regardless of duty status, is 24-hours per day, 365 days per year. The SGLI coverage may eventually be converted to a special Veterans' Group Life Insurance (VGLI) policy or to a commercial life insurance policy.

Family Servicemembers' Group Life Insurance (FSGLI) is a program providing low-cost coverage for spouses and dependent children of SGLI program members. FSGLI provides up to a maximum of $100,000 of insurance coverage for spouses (not to exceed the amount of SGLI the insured member has in force) and $10,000 for dependent children. Spousal coverage is issued in increments of $10,000 at a monthly cost ranging from $.55 to $5.20 per increment.

Survivor Benefits

When a service member dies, the Casualty Assistance Officer (CAO) is available to review the many benefits and entitlements available to surviving family members. The military offers a Death Gratuity in the form of a one-time non-taxable payment of $100,000 given to survivors of those whose deaths occur under the following conditions:

- A member of an armed force under his jurisdiction who dies while on active duty or while performing authorized travel to or from active duty;
- A Reserve of an armed force who dies while on inactive duty training (with exceptions);
- Any Reserve of an armed force who assumed an obligation to perform active duty for training, or inactive duty training (with exceptions) and who dies while traveling directly to or from that active duty for training or inactive duty training;
- Any member of a Reserve Officers' Training Corps who dies while performing annual training duty under orders for a period of more than 13 days, or while performing authorized travel to or from that annual training duty; or any applicant for membership in a Reserve Officers' Training Corps who dies while attending field training or a practice cruise or while performing authorized travel to or from the place where the training or cruise is conducted; or
- A person who dies while traveling to or from or while at a place for final acceptance, or for entry upon active duty (other than for training), in an armed force, who has been ordered or directed to go to that place, and who has been provisionally accepted for that duty; or has been selected for service in that armed force.

The death gratuity amount is made payable to survivors of the deceased in this order:

- The member's lawful surviving spouse.
- If there is no spouse, to the child or children of the member, regardless of age or marital status, in equal shares.
- If none of the above, then to the parents or brothers and/or sisters, or any combination as designated by the deceased member.

In addition, the VA provides partial reimbursement of an eligible veteran's burial and funeral costs for both service-related and non service-related deaths. For a service-related death, the VA will pay up to $2,000 toward burial expenses. If the veteran is buried in a VA national cemetery, some or all of the cost of transporting the deceased may also be reimbursed. In the case of a non service-related death, the VA will pay up to $300 toward burial and funeral expenses and a $300 plot-interment allowance. For eligibility requirements and application procedures, visit www.military.com/

Thrift Savings Plan

The Thrift Savings Plan (TSP) is a federal government-sponsored retirement savings and investment plan and offers the same type of savings and tax benefits that many private corporations offer their employees. The TSP is the military's version of a 401(k) plan. The biggest difference is that commercial firms that manage investment funds for 401(k)s typically impose annual fees from 50 cents to $1 per $100 in account balances. The military's TSP fees are around two cents per $100. Guardsmen can roll private sector 401(k) accounts into their TSP account where expenses are far lower than other rollover accounts. Reservists must be careful that combined contributions from periods of drill or active duty, and those made through other employer plans, don't exceed the annual 401(k) contribution limit of $15,500.

Bonuses

In the private sector, many companies offer bonus plans. There are signing bonuses given to new employees, retention bonuses for employees who make a long-term commitment to the company, and success bonuses given to employees who meet stated goals. There are also year-end bonuses where companies share profits with their employees. The Army has the same type of program for new recruits, enlisted members, and Officers. National Guard bonus/incentive programs change constantly. Current programs include, but are not limited to:

- Critical Skills MOS Bonus
- NGB Top Ten Critical Skills MOS Bonus
- Prior Service Enlistment Bonus
- Reenlistment/Extension Bonus

- Lump-sum payments, must successfully complete existing contractual obligations, effective on date of new contract, completion of training
- Enlisted Affiliation Bonus
- MOS Conversion Bonus

Be aware that as recruiting priorities change, bonuses will change and/or disappear. For more information, visit www.nationalguard.com.

Education

There are many educational benefits available for Guardsmen and their family members and the education benefits offered to Guardsmen were in for a major upgrade in 2009 under a new GI Bill. Most Guardsmen, mobilized since September 11, 2001, will be able to qualify for benefits under the new program.

The Army National Guard Education Support Center (ESC) is the centralized resource for education benefits for ARNG Soldiers, their dependents, and civilian employees of the ARNG. The ARNG ESC provides GI Bill eligibility analysis, educational counseling, degree planning, and various other educational services to Guardsmen and supplements the State Education Offices (which have information about education benefits specific to your state). To find out more information visit http://www.pec.ngb.army.mil/training/centers/esc/. As with bonuses, benefits are subject to change but here are some current National Guard education benefits:

- The Army National Guard Federal Tuition Assistance (FTA) Program provides financial assistance to part-time Soldiers in support of their professional and personal self-development goals. The ARNG is currently funding FTA at 100% of a member's tuition and authorized fees. Soldiers can use FTA for a variety of degrees including Secondary School Diploma or its equivalency; certificate (undergraduate, graduate, vocational, technical, licensure); associate; bachelor's (undergraduate); master's or first professional (graduate).
- The Montgomery GI Bill refers to various education assistance programs administered by the Department of Veterans Affairs for veterans, service members, and some dependents of disabled or

deceased veterans. Some Guard positions qualify for a GI Bill Kicker. The College Fund money, or "kicker," is an additional amount of money that increases an individual's basic Montgomery GI Bill monthly benefit and is included in his or her VA payment.

Space-A Travel

Space-A means flying on a space-available basis aboard military aircraft at little or no cost. This is a unique privilege provided to service members, retirees, and their families. Under the Space-A program, eligible passengers can fill unused seats on DoD-owned or controlled aircraft once all the space-required (duty) passengers and cargo have been accommodated. Air Mobility Command (AMC), based at Scott Air Force Base, manages the Air Force's worldwide airlift operations which includes the Space-A program.

Guardsmen on the Active Status List with identification may fly to, from, and between CONUS, Alaska, Hawaii, Puerto Rico, Guam, American Samoa, and the U.S. Virgin Islands. Additionally, when on active duty, members may fly anywhere overseas that AMC has flights operating. The most popular destinations are Europe and the Far East. If your Soldier is activated for more than 30 days (or if your Soldier is a full-time Guardsman), you have all the Space-A benefits of active duty members while you are on active duty ordinary leave (note that dependents can't travel unaccompanied). Typically, traditional Guard member dependents can't travel Space-A. If your sponsor becomes activated for more than 30 days, you have all the Space-A privileges of an active duty dependent accompanied by their sponsor on ordinary leave. Retired Guardsmen (including Gray Area retirees, those who are eligible for retirement pay at 60 years of age but are not yet 60 years old) and their family members can fly Space-A with proper paperwork. It's worth noting that S.542 has been introduced in the Senate. If it passes, reserve component members and their dependents will be able to travel Space-A on the same basis as the Active Component. For more information on Space-A travel, check out these websites:

- www.takeahop.org
- www.pepperd.com/vb/forum.php
- www.spacea.net

- www.militaryliving.com offers a number of comprehensive Space-A travel books/publications

Commissary, Exchange and Morale, Welfare and Recreation (MWR) Privileges

The Defense Commissary Agency operates a worldwide chain of nearly 275 commissaries, the civilian equivalent to a grocery store. Guard and authorized family members, with a valid military ID card, have unlimited commissary shopping privileges. Items are sold at cost plus a five-percent surcharge and shoppers can expect to save an average of 30 percent or more on their purchases compared to commercial prices. To find the commissary nearest you, visit www.commissaries.com. The Post Exchange, or PX for short, is the military version of a department store. There is no sales tax on merchandise and prices are usually well below commercial retailers. Check your local exchange to find out more www.aafes.com.

Army MWR www.armymwr.com is a comprehensive network of support and leisure services designed to enhance the lives of Soldiers and their families. MWR activities include on-base arts and crafts facilities, bowling centers, golf courses, libraries, outdoor recreation, recreation centers, youth services activities, and recreation membership clubs. Guard members and their dependents are entitled to use all class C facilities on the same basis as active duty personnel. Be sure to call ahead and confirm hours of operation and eligibility for the activity you and your family are interested in. From a Guard perspective, the best MWR perk is the ability to stay at the Armed Forces Recreation Centers:

- Virginia Beach, VA, www.capehenryinn.com Rates: $79+, Seasonal
- Germany, www.EdelweissLodgeandResort.com Rates: $84—$129
- Disney World, www.ShadesofGreen.org Rates: $80—$119 per night
- Hawaii, www.halekoa.com Rates: $79—$116 per night
- Korea, www.dragonhilllodge.com Rates: $59—$82 per night

These full-service resort hotels provide an affordable vacation experience for military families. Be warned, they book very far in advance. If your family wants to visit Disney World, the sooner you book the better. Rooms are booked up to a year in advance. If you are traveling to other locations, temporary military lodging includes 22,000 Army lodging units, temporary housing, and guesthouses at 80 locations in the United States, Korea, Japan, Belgium, Germany, Italy, Alaska, and Hawaii. They can all be reached with one toll-free call: 1-800-GO-ARMY-1 (1-800-462-7691).

There is also a program called the Lodging Success Program (LSP), which offers special rates for hotels located near Army installations. This program offers hotels in Atlanta, San Antonio, the National Capital Region, Hampton, Newport News, Miami, and Puerto Rico. To make reservations contact 1-866-Do DLSP1 (1-866-363-5771) or e-mail reservations at central reservations@redstone.army.mil.

Wrap Up:

- To connect to benefits, a Soldier and his or her dependents must be registered in DEERS. Any major changes such as marriage, divorce, or birth of a child must be reported to DEERS immediately.
- The Common Access Card (CAC) is your Soldier's passport to military facilities and systems. A spouse's military identification card gives them access to private-sector perks and military privileges such as shopping at the PX or commissary.
- A Soldier's compensation package includes his or her paycheck, retirement pension, health/dental insurance, and life insurance. All of these help position your family for long-term financial success.
- When Soldiers are activated under Title 10, they receive,

START SPREADING THE NEWS

Established in 1919, the Soldiers', Sailors', Marines', Coast Guard, and Airmen's' Club of New York City provides a safe, comfortable, and affordable place for military families to stay when visiting the Big Apple. This townhouse-style facility is conveniently located at 37th and Lexington in a very nice neighborhood and rents individual beds instead of rooms. However, if you, your spouse, and children need four beds, you'll probably be assigned a room for four. The Club's common areas include the canteen, two lounges, and a library with televisions, VCRs, and DVD units. Rates are $20-$90 depending on rank and accommodations. Retirees are welcome too! www.ssmaclub.org.

as do their family members, the same benefits and entitlements as their active duty counterparts.

- Many Guardsmen are eligible for robust bonuses and money for education. These perks are always changing but are easy to track on the web or through your state's education and recruitment offices.
- Guard family members are entitled to full commissary, exchange, and MWR privileges. These perks can save your family thousands of dollars a year and give you a chance to relax and enjoy the fruits of Guard life.

Chapter 8

The Guard Family

The Guard Family

The National Guard family includes what you might expect: the Soldier, his or her spouse, children, parents, extended family members, and friends. In addition, the Guard family includes community members and organizations who want to support our Soldiers. The Guard family does not exist to send care packages to deployed Soldiers (although this is nice); it exists to unify all members in support of their Soldier and make sure that we are on the same page. Our mission is to be at the ready for anything and everything that comes our way. We must be ready for every type of mission, whether a stateside emergency or a long deployment overseas.

In my years of being a military wife, I am still amazed at the number of dedicated members of the Guard Family who spend countless volunteer hours to support our Soldiers. They volunteer for their Family Readiness Group (FRG), coordinate care packages for deployed Soldiers, plan activities and events, and provide childcare services at professional conferences. They ask the companies they work for, as well as other businesses, to donate goods and services to raffle away at the annual company party. Or, they spend hours and hours of their own time creating something beautiful for a lucky conference attendee who holds the magic ticket. Some people write newsletters. Some people create websites. Some people plant flowers in front of the armory. Some pick up the phone and call the spouse of a deployed Soldier to see how they are and if they need anything. Whatever they do and however they choose to share their resources, time, and talent, they do it because they love their Soldier and they love the Guard. I think this is wonderful, especially in the Citizen-Soldier world where it is easy to fly under the radar and escape notice.

But I want to make one thing clear: if you support your Soldier's commitment to serve our country, you are doing enough. Take care of yourself, take care of your family, and the Army will take care of the Soldier. If, however, you want to get involved, there are many opportunities to do so and I know that you will find it very rewarding. There are many outlets to volunteer and you can easily find a way to contribute that fits into your own busy schedule.

Being involved in the Guard family is a fun way to bond with your Soldier. The happiest Soldiers I know have a supportive family standing by their side. It is also a great way to meet new friends. You will feel instantly connected to other members of the Guard family. Nine times out of ten, you will hit it off with the people who you meet simply because we share something so big and so important. Even if you don't see them often, when you do, you will pick up right where you left off. It is hard to explain. But if you have been in the Guard family for awhile, you don't need an explanation. You know exactly what I mean.

The Big Three Family Program Resources

The National Guard launched a powerful new website that provides direction for all things concerning the family: www.guardfamily.org. This website will provide the information you need to get in touch with your local resources. To summarize, the National Guard provides a powerful trio of state-based organizations to Guard families:

- The State Family Programs Office (SFPO): Provides assistance, guidance, and support to Guard members and their families.
- Family Assistance Centers (FAC): Provides essential family services via referral during a major deployment.
- Family Readiness Groups (FRG): Provides family members with a unitlevel connection to their Soldiers and the Army whether Soldiers are home or on a deployment.

All of these groups work together from the top down. They all have different charters, but work together to create, maintain, and improve programs and resources that benefit our families. Their goal is to harness information from all sources and distribute it at the most finite level possible. If you can't find the information that you need online, I can guarantee you that a phone call or e-mail to your SFPO, FAC, or FRG will get you moving in the right direction.

The State Family Programs Office (SFPO): A Full-Time Family Resource

Every state has a SFPO run by full-time staff members. The SFPO coordinator is responsible for maintaining regular contact with the AG, the National Guard Bureau, and, most importantly, individual unit FRGs. While each state's program mission and priorities vary, the following list represents the typical charter for the SFPO:

- Develop and support unit Family Readiness Groups (FRGs).
- Coordinate Guard Youth programs, camps, and symposiums.
- Increase the knowledge of family members regarding the benefits, privileges, and obligations of Guard service.
- Evaluate family needs and devise strategies to meet both short-term and long-term needs.
- Serve as the conduit between the National Guard Bureau, state military, veteran's affairs organizations, and the National Guard Family.
- Create a family support system to assist members during separation.
- Provide information/referral networking.
- Enhance Guard retention by taking care of Guard members and their family members.
- Provide feedback to the Command on the family member concerns.

The SFPO is also a good referral source to special family support programs, family member readiness training, and educational materials. Depending on where you live, you may or may not interface with the folks in the SFPO. In smaller states, they may contact every family monthly to reach out and connect as well as inform them of upcoming activities. In other states, you will only see SFPO representatives at pre-deployment sessions held at the armory. Either way, they are a resource for you and can be reached via telephone or e-mailed during business hours. Their contact information will be listed on your state Guard organization website or under the resource locater at www.guardfamily.org. If you have a question or concern and don't know where to start, start with your SFPO. I have always found the people at the SFPO to be extremely friendly and resourceful. If they don't have the information that you need, they will point you in the right direction.

Family Assistance Centers (FAC's): A Dedicated Resource for Family Members When Soldiers are Deployed

There are more than 300 Family Assistance Centers (FACs) across 54 states and territories that provide information, referral, and outreach to military families. FACs are particularly useful to geographically-disbursed National Guard families. Although they are always available, Family Assistance Centers are a key player during mobilization and demobilization of units. When Guard units are deployed, the SFPO is a coordinating agency for the operation of Family Assistance Centers (FACs) located throughout each state. FACs have a singular focus—provide a one-stop-shop for the families of mobilized Soldiers. FACs are usually formed to support major deployments and are opened and closed according to need. FAC workers are paid employees of the state and have set office hours. They work closely with FAC volunteers and are available via cell phone 24/7. A FAC employee will either help you resolve your issue or direct you to the appropriate agency that can help you with your specific need. FACs are located in strategic locations throughout each state and are frequently housed at armories. FAC locations are listed on each state's individual Guard website and at www.jointservicessupport.com. Each FAC is linked directly to Rear Detachment Command (RDC) and the SFPO.

FAC employees are a very proactive and enthusiastic group. When a Soldier deploys, it is likely that they will contact the primary point of contact to make sure you have their contact information and understand what they can do for you. If you don't hear from your local FAC, pick up the phone and call them! They want to hear from you and make sure that you are in the system and being taken care of. Keep in mind that the FAC is there to assist any member of the Guard family. This is an excellent resource for parents and extended family members. You can get FAC assistance by visiting during office hours, sending an e-mail, or making a phone call.

The FAC serves as a central command to ensure that families are receiving accurate and timely assistance, as well as the information they need throughout the separation. FACs specialize in the following:

- TRICARE assistance
- Defense Enrollment Eligibility Reporting System (DEERS) enrollment and information
- Legal resources and referral
- Pay issues
- Financial counseling/training
- Resources for community support
- Emergency assistance coordination (including financial assistance)
- Issuance of ID cards. Crisis intervention and referral
- Supporting/Mentoring Family Readiness Groups

Not sure how your medical benefits work? Lose your military ID and not sure what to do about it? Receive a call from a reporter asking about National Guard business? Know of a Guard family that is having severe financial difficulty? Want to know of other military families in your specific community? Kids need a fun night out and wondering if there are any discount tickets, to the circus or nearest theme park? Call your FAC.

Every FAC's goal is to solve problems as quickly as possible. But that does not mean that they are the ones who actually provide the assistance. They don't have lawyers and counselors on staff, but they can help locate one for you. They can't write you a check to solve a financial problem, but they know about programs (some sponsored by the military, some sponsored

Family Assistance Web Sites/Programs:

- Army Families Online www.armyfamiliesonline.org
- The Department of Defense (DoD) Military OneSource Program www.militaryonesource.com
- DoD MilitaryHOMEFRONT web portal www.militaryhomefront. dod.mil
- Operation Purple www.NMFA.org

by your state, some sponsored by private organizations or individuals) for which you may qualify to get aid. They are not going to show up at your house and clean your gutters or shovel snow, but if there is an American Legion or another group in your area that provides this service, they will know about it. More than anything else, FACs are really an information and referral agency. To locate your nearest FAC, visit www.guardfamily.org.

The Family Readiness Group: Your Unit-Level Connection

The third, and most vital, component of the family programs trio is the Family Readiness Group (FRG). As we discussed in "What if Your Spouse is the Company Commander," FRGs are formed at the unit-level and are the bond that hold our families together whether our Soldiers are home or abroad. They are the conduit to vital information that can help families. Most importantly, FRGs help lessen the feeling of isolation that we may feel as members of the Citizen-Soldier community. FRG leaders work directly with the unit's company commander and the SFPO. This ensures that information is flowing in real time and helps create a strong supportive family network.

Pre 9/11, FRGs were most often associated with planning social events and programs for family members. And while it is true that the FRG still plans most social events, they do so much more. Perhaps you receive a quarterly newsletter to keep you abreast of unit activities. You may have heard the term phone tree tossed about here and there and received a test call to make sure your contact information was up-to-date. All of these initiatives are carried out by your unit's FRG.

FRGs are your local connection to the Guard organization and Guard family and put a friendly face on what can sometimes feel like a very large and bureaucratic organization. FRGs are formed at the unit level. Each has its own unique personality and their goals are specific to the particular unit that they support. Some units have longstanding, active, efficient FRGs that hold regular meetings and boast a large membership. Other units are reinvigorating or re-launching their FRG and are focused on recruiting volunteers to build an organization from the ground up. Every FRG must have an official charter (or be filling out the paperwork to obtain one) and exist to support Guard families (whether Soldiers are home or deployed) and plan events/programs that benefit the entire FRG membership. The FRG is the first component of your personal readiness support network.

That's right; the FRGs most important role has to do with the "R" part of their title. Their mission is to make sure we are ready for whatever comes our way. Guard Soldiers must be prepared to serve at a moment's notice. And when they leave, whether for a month of state duty or a year overseas, our lives get complicated. When they are called to duty, we are also called to duty and must be ready to snap into military mode.

The Company Commander: Where the Buck Stops for Family Readiness

Just as the Guard family begins with the Soldier, so does FRG membership. The FRG isn't a wives group that gets together once a year to plan a holiday party or organize care packages. Family Readiness is part of every unit's discipline. It is as important as anything else that the unit does. That is why every Soldier is a member of the unit's FRG. And, that is why, even though the company commander does not lead the FRG, he or she is responsible for making sure the unit has an active, viable FRG in place. In the same way that the Soldier is the center of the Guard family, the company commander is responsible for implementing and maintaining a healthy and energized FRG. An incoming commander should immediately determine if a functioning FRG exists. A functioning FRG will include an active and identifiable FRG leader. If there is an FRG leader in place, the commander should meet with that person as soon as possible. A smart commander will contact the FRG leader and introduce himself/herself before the official change-of-command ceremony. Ideally, the incoming commander should meet with the FRG leadership in person to determine:

- What type of support the FRG has in place (i.e., number of active volunteers). Any past issues that may affect the quality of the FRG moving forward.
- The FRG leader's preferred method of communication (e-mail, phone, or face-to-face meetings in the armory).
- Any official training or educational programs that the FRG leader should attend.
- Any pending or planned programs/activities that are on the unit calendar or need to be put on the unit calendar.

If the commander is married, this is a good time to figure out the best role his or her spouse might play in the FRG. Some FRGs expect a lot of involvement from the commander's spouse, others just want the spouse to support the FRG in a background role.

No matter what role his or her spouse plays in the company FRG, the commander must give the FRG leader an ongoing commitment and his or her support. If an active FRG does not exist, it is the commander's responsibility to create one from the ground up. No matter what the status of the FRG, the commander needs to appoint a Guard member as the point of contact to focus on family readiness issues. This Soldier is the liaison between the commander and the FRG. This Soldier interfaces with the FRG leader and gives this person access to all of the equipment, supplies, and personnel necessary to get their job done. This Soldier can be a member of the leadership team such as an NCO or Lieutenant or any member of the unit who shows interest in this position. If you are married to a Soldier who wants to heighten his or her profile within the company, this is an excellent way to get noticed by the commander. Encourage your Soldier to approach the commander and ask to be involved in family programs.

Commanders should consider both the Soldier point of contact and FRG leader as part of their staff and can include them in briefings with his or her leadership team. At a minimum, the commander needs to keep in close touch with the FRG leader via phone or e-mail and make sure he is aware of any family program issues and activities. Most states sponsor annual Family Readiness Conferences. Commanders, their spouses, unit FRG leaders, and other significant personnel are invited to attend this training event. The Army covers expenses such as travel and lodging. Civilian FRG leaders are usually put on official orders for these events.

FRG Focus When Soldiers are Home

If you are a new FRG leader and don't know where to start, or a Guard supporter who wants to help out the unit's FRG, here are four good things to focus on when the Soldiers are home:

1. Establishing a regular meeting time at a convenient location and/or set up a virtual FRG (explanation below).
2. Creating and maintaining an accurate, updated unit telephone tree.
3. Communicating to families using other outreach programs.

4. Planning events and programs that all Guard families will attend and
   enjoy

The FRG Leader:
The Volunteer Who Makes it All Happen

The FRG leader is the commander's representative for all family-related training, programs, and events. The FRG leader guides and directs a network of volunteers according to the rules and regulations set forth by the Army. Even though she is a volunteer, the FRG leader has a job description, attends training sessions, and is accountable to the unit and the SFPO. An FRG leader can expect to spend from five to fifteen hours a month doing FRG activities (many spend much more time than this!)

A GUARD FRG LEADER

- Loves the unit and believes that the FRG is vital to the organization
- Has a great attitude and remains positive—even in the face of adversity
- Is a quick study and can process a lot of information simultaneously
- Is proactive, creative, and organized
- Doesn't take things personally
- Is accessible and visible to Soldiers and their families
- Can keep a confidence and avoids gossip

If you are interested in becoming an FRG leader, get involved with your FRG group and learn the ropes. If your unit does not have an active FRG, let the commander know that you are interested. It is a demanding position but also very worthwhile. Also, being an FRG leader (or volunteer) is certainly something that you can put on your resume and leverage in your civilian career.

And to all of the FRG leaders out there, thank you for your service. Know that you are the FRG's best recruiting tool. Good people attract good people. But it can take time to get a team in place. Be patient and continue to move forward. Take baby steps and do the best that you can. Even if your FRG is just you and another go-getter, you have the right foundation to build an effective FRG. Set reasonable goals and concentrate on providing a basic level of service. It is much better to focus and excel at a few things than to take on too much and drop the ball or become discouraged.

FRG Meetings

If your unit FRG has an active in-person membership, that is outstanding! Keep doing what you are doing. Regular meetings are necessary to set FRG goals and meet FRG goals. If you struggle getting people to attend meetings, you are not alone. Establishing a vibrant in-person FRG is a challenge in the Guard due to logistics. Whether soldiers are deployed or home, it makes sense to "bundle" FRG meeting with other events. For example, have an onsite FRG meeting an hour prior to the annual holiday party or a care package event. This is a great way to maximize attendance.

Luckily, technology has helped bridge the distance between Guard family members. A convenient option to keep in touch, communicate timely information, and move programs forward is a Virtual Family Readiness Group (vFRG). Basically, a vFRG is a secure website containing information pertinent to unit family members. Unlike public websites, Operational Security (OPSEC) is the number one priority for vFRGs.

Virtual Family Readiness Group (vFRG)

Virtual Family Readiness Groups are set up at www.armyfrg.org. This new portal provides all of the functionality of a traditional FRG—online. A vFRG allows Soldiers, spouses, and extended family members safe, secure access to information from any location.

The website www.armyfrg.org is maintained and updated by the Army and is used by both regular Army and National Guard commanders. To get started, the company commander and FRG leader must register their FRG at www.armyfrg.org. The vFRG is currently set up for battalion-level organizations but units can be given an exception to set up a website. This must be done through the unit commander. The registration and approval process requires information specific to the unit. Approval is sent via e-mail and, at this point, the commander and FRG leader can start populating the website. To ensure that the FRG leader and commander are committed to the long-term success of the vFRG, before a site goes live, a minimum amount of information must be entered.

Once the basic website is activated, the next step is to populate the Soldier database with all unit members. In order for a family member to subscribe to a vFRG, the Soldier must be in the Soldier database for his or her FRG first and enter the family member into an invitation list. It is important to note that the family member's name must appear exactly as it was entered in the invitation list for automatic approval and the Soldier's name must appear exactly as it was entered into the Soldier Database. Once they are on the official list, family members must register at www.armyfrg.org by providing their name, sponsoring Soldier's name, and the last four digits of the Soldier's Social Security Number. The information provided will be authenticated by command level administrators and an approval notice sent out. After they are approved, users can go into the system and sign up as a member for their unit's vFRG. Upon entry to the vFRGs members can browse to their individual unit site by clicking on the "Find an FRG" link.

Army Knowledge Online (AKO)

Another tool available free-of-charge to all Guard family members is the Army Knowledge Online (AKO). AKO is the Army's version of secure e-mail/internet. It allows service members and designated civilian family members (i.e., FRG leaders, commander's spouse, and other FRG members as appropriate) free online access 24 hours a day/7 days a week via a secure connection. It also has instant messaging capability. AKO assures OPSEC. A Soldier can authorize friends and family members for AKO guest accounts. Unit family members can request a guest account from the AKO home page and the Soldier will receive an e-mail asking for his approval of the account. AKO is a great place to begin building an online FRG community for a unit, especially if the unit does not have a vFRG. AKO provides private family team sites with restricted access and chat areas to hold a virtual meeting with FRG members. Keep in mind that if a chat feature is added, it should be a member-only forum with assigned passwords. All entries and posts need to be closely monitored to prevent gossip and ensure that all information is unclassified. Every FRG Leader should take the time to familiarize themselves with vFRG and AKO and deploy these tools to maximize their reach to family members.

The Telephone Tree

The "Telephone Tree," sometimes called "The Chain of Concern," is a system that allows important messages to be relayed to family members as quickly and accurately as possible. Reasons for using the tree can range anywhere from planning social functions to relaying emergency information. The tree is the tool the Army uses to pass on accurate, clear, concise, and approved messages. It allows everybody to be on the same page and helps minimize rumors. Different units use different methods to create and maintain their tree. The FRG usually distributes a questionnaire to family members. Spouses provide basic contact information and indicate any contact caveats (such as hours where they can be reached in each location and preferred number where they can be reached). Spouses should have the choice of having their information posted on a general roster or reserved on the confidential roster that is given only to the FRG leader. The questionnaire must include a firm statement assuring that the roster may not be used for any non-official business (such as recruitment for business parties like Mary Kay®, Tupperware®, etc.). Once the tree is complete, a privacy statement should be printed on every type of roster. The general roster can be distributed to unit family members and posted on the vFRG.

Here's how it works: Family members are ordered on a branch. The top family member of each branch is the Key Caller. The Key Caller will receive a message from the FRG leader. They, in turn, will call each family member on the chain below them. In the Guard, however, a unit usually designates key members of the organization (i.e., the FRG leader, commander's wife, the military POC, and other volunteers) to contact a designated number of family members. It is important to recruit enough reliable callers to ensure that every family is called and that a few people are not stuck making dozens of phone calls to family members.

Typically, the FRG leader will be asked by the commander to start the chain and call the first person on the list. They will work together to craft a written statement that relays all of the necessary information. This script is short, specific, and outlines all the information that needs to be relayed. The goal is to minimize questions so the team can contact all family members in a timely way. The documented script should be distributed to other callers via e-mail. The message should contain the five Ws: Who, What, When, Where, and Why? Here is an example of utilizing the telephone tree during annual training:

Situation:
The unit has been delayed a day in their return home. The FRG leader is notified. He or she calls the telephone tree POC and the message is passed on until all are contacted. The official message reads:

Script:
"The (unit name) has been delayed 24 hours because of a change in air flight schedules. The unit will return to the armory at _____ (time) on _____ (day of week, date). Please notify your family members of the delay. If you need further information, call (name and phone number)."

Keeping rosters updated is an ongoing requirement and is especially important during deployments. The best way to make sure the tree is working is to test it periodically when Soldiers are home to ensure accuracy of information. It is also an excellent tool to have when you are planning and managing company events. You never know when plans will change. And if you have to reach 100 people in a matter of hours, an up-to-date telephone tree is the only way to accomplish that mission. If you are a friendly, organized, and detail-oriented person, consider volunteering to help with the telephone tree. You can help compile information, update or maintain it. If you are pressed for time, consider volunteering to serve as a caller when the tree is activated.

Two Key Things to Remember About the Telephone Tree

- Don't be alarmed if you receive a telephone tree call. If your Soldier is deployed, the tree is used to communicate all types of information including events/ activities or news. The tree is NEVER used to inform family members about injuries or accidents and it is NEVER used for death notifications.

- The telephone tree is an official process. It should only be used to communicate information that has been approved by the commander. The tree ensures that families receive accurate and consistent information. If you don't hear it from the tree, it should be considered hearsay or a rumor.

Other Types of Outreach

Newsletters

Newsletters are a great way to reach everybody in the company. For those who have been in the company for a while, an informative e-newsletter or a simple family news flyer copied on colored paper and sent home with the Soldier every drill shows that the unit values family members and wants to keep them informed. No matter how involved a Soldier is with their unit or what their rank, family members are always happy to hear unit news. Taking the time to put together a quarterly newsletter or monthly announcement shows that the commander and FRG are organized and active. Hopefully, this will be the catalyst for future involvement. The purpose of an FRG newsletter is to help families understand the unit's mission and keep families informed about the benefits and resources available to them. Newsletters promote family readiness and camaraderie. FRG newsletters must follow specific regulations and procedures and every unit FRG will have a Memorandum of Inspection (MOI) or Standing Operating Procedure (SOP) that provides instructions for preparing, printing, and distributing official newsletters. Be aware that there are page limitations and other rules governing official FRG newsletters (see AR 25-30, The Army Integrated Publishing and Printing Program for more information. It is available online). Newsletters contain both official and unofficial information. Official information includes command and mission-essential information that the commander would like families to know about (i.e., FRG-sponsored activities, resources, programs, and services). Unofficial information includes non-mission related items (i.e., photos, coloring pages, birth announcements, etc.) Official military mail may be used for distribution of official FRG correspondence. If the newsletter is an unofficial publication, it should be mailed using FRG funds. Either way, the commander needs to approve any correspondence before it is distributed to membership.

DON'T include want ads, fundraising activities done by outside organizations, invitations to personal events, personal information (such as addresses), or any FRG financial information.

In my ideal world, I would receive a gorgeous newsletter (carefully balancing the perfect amount of white space with a fair amount of full-color photography) in my mailbox every month. That way, I could peruse it at my

IDEAS FOR FRG NEWSLETTER CONTENT

- Commander's Corner
- FRG Leader's Corner
- First Sergeant's Corner
- FRG meeting information or call for volunteers
- Upcoming unit event dates
- Mark your calendar for any family program events, unit drills, or training
- Countdown to AT
- Information on benefits
- Welcome to new families
- Updates in military regulations that impact family members' interest pertaining to the National Guard
- Unit facts and history
- Chain of command contact information or photos
- Pre-deployment and deployment information
- FAC locations
- Kid's coloring pages
- Recipes
- Highlights and photos of past FRG events
- Soldier or spouse-of-the-month profile

leisure poolside or over a cup of chamomile tea. However, sending newsletters through the mail is expensive. With all the junk mail nowadays, it could easily end up in the recycling bin. Many units send newsletters to Soldiers and their spouses via e-mail. I think this works well. If the FRG does not have the time or resources to publish a monthly or quarterly newsletter, they should ask for some space in the unit's monthly newsletter. This can be supplemented with a one-page, monthly flyer that is handed out during drill (and posted on the backside of the bathroom stall doors at the armory . . . they will not escape notice there!). Services such as www.MailChimp.com are the perfect way to stay in touch with unit family members who elect to provide their e-mails. Online newsletter services offer fun templates and allow recipients to unsubscribe. They also make it easy to track if the newsletter is actually being opened and read. Just be sure not to include any classified information in a newsletter.

Armory Bulletin Board

Your Soldier's unit will have a bulletin board where official unit information is posted. This will include things like drill schedules, commander's policy letters, uniform updates, and job opportunities. Ask the commander for a place to display information pertaining to families.

A Family Information Board is a nice way to tell Soldiers and visiting family members about benefits, activities, and unit accomplishments. I always enjoy seeing photos from deployments, award ceremonies, and family events. I also like to see information on the unit's history such as historical photographs. An updated bulletin board is a great addition to a family day and also a good opportunity to show off for visiting battalion leadership.

Welcome Packets

New Soldier in-processing is a requirement in every unit. When a new Soldier reports for their first drill, they will be shown the ropes by a unit representative as designated by the First Sergeant. There is so much to cover that the details of the FRG may be glossed over. This is a huge opportunity! Why not put together an official, attractive Welcome Packet for the Soldier to take home to his or her family? Well, because your cute folders will sit in the corner of the armory and eventually get lost in the circa 1950 Steelcase file drawer never to be seen again!

A better idea is to print up a one page "Fridge Facts" sheet on astro bright paper that will stand out among the sea of generic white, 8.5 x 11 sheets. These can be stacked around the orderly room of the armory. The Fridge Facts sheet summarizes all key unit/FRG information on one sheet:

- A list, by month, of key dates (monthly drill, AT, battalion events)
- A list of your FRG events
- Contact information for commander, First Sergeant, their spouses if they are involved in the FRG, and the FRG Leader
- Armory address and phone number
- Key URLs including the unit website and vFRG

Print out 20 copies of the Fridge Facts for the full-time Readiness NCO. Keep the information updated and accessible.

Family Events

To recruit volunteers, people need to know that the FRG exists and see the value. When Soldiers are home the best way to promote the FRG is to plan family events that ALL Soldiers can participate in and enjoy. It is very important to keep Soldiers and couples without children in mind when making plans. For example, if there is a kid-specific event at the armory or elsewhere, have something else for single Soldiers and those without

Unit Family Programs Survey-Check one:

I am:
_____Single
_____Single with significant other
_____Single with children
_____Married with children
_____Married without children

Rank each of the following events from 1-5. One means that you are "unlikely to attend," Five means that you are "very likely to attend."

_____Adults-only, formal appetizer/cocktail buffet at a local venue. $15-$20 per person.
_____Adults-only, formal sit-down dinner at a local venue. $25-$35 per person.
_____Informal family holiday party in armory with children's events and alternative events for those who don't have children. Free.
_____Summer picnic at park located in a centralized location with children's events and alternative events for those who don't have children. Free.
_____Sporting event/amusement park/day trip with discounted tickets.

Other suggestions:

Rank each of the following incentives to attend a unit event 1-5. One means that it isn't an incentive. Five means that it is a STRONG incentive:

_____Informal day time event held off-site
_____Informal day time event held in armory
_____Formal evening event
_____Event held in central location for unit members
_____Event held over drill weekend
_____On-site childcare provided
_____Free food/beverages

children. Group activities give the members of the unit and their spouses and families the opportunity to have fun and bond as a group. Examples of popular events include: spouse gatherings, parties, picnics, and community open houses. We all have different preferences for the type of events that we like to attend. Of course, you can't please everyone, but the goal is to cast the widest net possible. The best way to find out what types of programs/events that Soldiers and their family members are likely to attend is to ask them. The incoming company commander should distribute a survey to Soldiers on a drill weekend. Soldiers should be given time to call their spouses or significant others to get their input as well. The survey is anonymous and does not need to be long or complicated. In fact, it only needs to include the items shown in the sample survey on the previous page.

All Soldiers including leadership need to complete the survey and return it by the end of drill. The survey results will give the commander and FRG leader a good idea about what type of events will benefit the majority of the unit. Tackle one or two major events per year that the majority of people will attend and enjoy. Use the data to be creative. For example, if only 20 people in the unit have a strong interest in attending a formal event, you may consider combining efforts with another unit or buying a block of tables at a battalion or brigade formal that is already in the works. If five people in the unit are excited about free tickets to a theme park or sporting event, call your SFPO and see if they have a few complimentary tickets available or call the community relations people at the park and give them an opportunity to support the military.

Other FRG Opportunities

Family Readiness Groups do much more than the initiatives highlighted in this chapter. Here are a few other key focus areas when Soldiers are home:

- Keeping in touch with family members
- Networking with other FRGs and staying updated on any FRG policy changes
- Attending official training programs to stay abreast of changes that affect families (Tricare, military pay, readiness training, re-enlistment, or retirement briefings, etc.)
- Adopting a deployed unit
- Community outreach

- Leveraging technology to make the FRG more accessible (virtual family readiness groups)

The most important thing an FRG does when Soldiers are home is prepare families for possible deployment. They are always focused on the "R." They always want families to be ready. An FRG that holds regular meetings, communicates with families, and sponsors family events is well-positioned to support families during a deployment. All of the activities we have discussed provide a support infrastructure.

When Soldiers deploy, the FRG springs to action and takes on a long-term, more constant role. The FRG will focus on:

- Keeping in touch with family members of deployed Soldiers via e-mail, phone, written publications, and planned activities. During a deployment, FRG outreach will expand to include extended family members who wish to stay in the loop.
- Serving as a referral agency to family members who are having difficulties (financial, health problems, domestic issues, etc.) or need information. The FRG will work closely with the FPO and closest FAC to make sure needs are addressed.
- Reaching out to the private sector/local community to get their involvement and support for members of the Guard family. Initiatives may include finding sponsors to underwrite the cost of care packages or sponsoring a Spouses Night Out.
- Working with the Chaplain's office to handle crisis situations. Battalion/unit leadership will communicate directly with the FRG leader and determine the FRGs role during and after a crisis i.e., death of Soldier or family member. In this situation, the FRG may be called upon in the short-term to distribute information such as funeral arrangements to unit families and coordinate support such as providing meals for the bereaved family.

Of course, when the unit returns, the FRG's focus will shift again. If Soldiers were injured or killed during a deployment, the unit will focus on providing long-term outreach to their families. They may sponsor programs to help families adjust to homecoming letdown and educate concerned family members about the complexity of Post Traumatic Stress Disorder.

When families have had time to readjust and enjoy some time together, they may adopt another unit that is deploying. The FRG's mission will really depend on the unit's state of mind. It is likely that the FRG will pull back after a deployment. This is only natural. After months of working overtime, the FRG members (and especially the FRG leader) deserve a break. Even though FRG leaders seem like they can take on the world, they have their own families to take care of. After months of separation, every family needs some private time to allow Soldiers to reintegrate into their family and get re-situated in their civilian jobs. The good news is that a well-run FRG transitions easily into a non-deployed status. The friendships formed during the deployment will fuel the FRG as it shifts its focus back to business as usual.

How Do I Get Involved?

Family Readiness Groups are like any other volunteer organization. Some people do a lot, some do enough, and some people don't do anything. Just in the same way that some people sign up to bring the plastic forks and juice bags and some people make the sandwiches and bake the cupcakes. I don't think this is intentional; I just think people are

---

Yellow Ribbon Reintegration Program

The legislatively mandated Yellow Ribbon Reintegration Program www.jointservicessupport.org/YRRP provides outreach to National Guard and Reserve service members, their families, communities, and employers throughout all phases of the deployment cycle. Services include:

- Anger, substance abuse, domestic violence awareness/management
- Child Care Services
- Community Relations
- Employer Support for the Guard and Reserve (ESGR)
- Employment opportunities
- Family Counseling Referral/ Marriage Enrichment Programs/ Child Behavioral Referral
- Financial Counseling Referral
- Legal Counseling Referral
- Preparations for reintegration
- School Support
- Single Service member issues/ support
- Traumatic Brain Injury Information and Support
- TRICARE Medical Benefits/ Dental Benefits (while deployed and upon return)
- Veterans Affairs Information/ Veterans Benefits Information
- Warrior Transition Unit Information

really, really busy. If every family member and extended member offered to do one small thing a year, it would make a big difference to our FRGs. Even if your unit is two hours away, even if you don't have the time to commit to long-term involvement, even if you only have a few hours to give, there is a place for you in your unit FRG. The internet, e-mail, and social networking sites such as Facebook and Twitter have made it possible to be involved without having to leave the comfort of your own home.

FRG leaders will take any time that you have to offer and nobody is going to make you go to meetings or do things that don't interest you or that you have no time to offer. Your unit FRG will be grateful for any help.

If you love to scrapbook, volunteer to put together the Family Bulletin Board. If you are a great writer, get in touch with the FRG leader and offer to write an article for the unit newsletter. If photography is your passion, offer to take photographs at company events and post them on the vFRG or volunteer to put together a slide show for the annual Dining Out. If you like to surf the internet, work with the newsletter or website team and submit short articles that would be of interest to the family members in your unit such as military traditions and etiquette, Guard benefits, program information, etc. If you have connections, offer to solicit donations for an upcoming event or care package initiative. If you are good with details and follow-up, offer your assistance with the telephone tree. If you love to decorate, cook, and entertain, get involved with unit events. Design the invitations, centerpieces, or programs. Help with menu selections. Suggest possible themes. If you are a natural organizer, offer to assemble invitations, track RSVPs, or coordinate with vendors. If you are an out-of-the-box thinker, come up with the evening entertainment. (We did Family Feud at our unit holiday party. Each team included an Officer, NCO, private, spouse, and community member/retired Guardsman. It was hilarious.) If you are a musician, offer to provide background music during dinner. If you have no qualms about asking people for things and have good connections, offer to solicit donations for door prizes—just be sure to check with the FRG leader to make sure you are following the regulations pertaining to fundraising and donations. If you are a great bargain shopper, get some funds allocated from the FRG so you can hunt down items and assemble beautiful gift baskets for door prizes. There is something for everybody in your FRG.

One "ah ha" thing that I have learned recently is that you can be involved in any FRG that you choose. If your Soldier's unit is two hours away, you can get involved with an FRG near your home. Get in touch with your SFPO to find out the closest unit. In this scenario, you have the best of both worlds: you will still be included in your home FRG's communication network i.e., keeping in touch via e-mail and telephone but you can attend regular meetings and events closer to home. This convenient option lets you have the face-to-face connection without the long commute. The ideal time to get involved with the unit FRG is when our Soldiers are home. If you have not had a chance to meet people in the unit, ask your Soldier to introduce you to the FRG leader and other family members. If your Soldier is deployed, get in touch with the FRG leader directly. This ensures that you will be informed about upcoming programs and events. Even a tiny bit of involvement in your FRG will pay big dividends. The biggest payback is the friendships that you will build. Even if you have a few Guard friends who you stay in touch with, don't ever rest on your laurels. It is very easy to get comfortable with the friends that you have made within a particular unit. Certainly, we all have our favorites. But why limit yourself? If your Soldier changes units, be sure to reach out to the FRG leader and other family members. If they change units again, simply rinse and repeat!

Keep in touch with your old friends but reach out and meet new people. It is ideal to always have friends in your unit and friends in other units, as well. That way, you can take turns supporting each other when one or the other of your Soldiers deploy. The more people you know, the bigger support network you will have. And when your Soldier deploys, you are going to want to have Guard friends, both old and new, who you can lean on.

Wrap Up

- The National Guard family starts with the Soldier. We are here for them and they must be here for us. They are your connection to family programs. Hold them accountable.
- Knowledge is power! Your SFPO and FAC are your connection to all of the information and resources available. Tap into their expertise.
- Find the closest FRG and get involved. Every FRG wants new faces. Don't worry, you will not be asked to do anything more than you want.
- When Soldiers are home, there are specific ways to use your talent to help the FRG. Even if you live far from the armory, there are things that you can do virtually.
- If you don't have an active FRG in your unit or don't know anything about your FRG, it is never too late to get involved!

Chapter 9

Official Guard Functions

In the Army, there are many opportunities to socialize with other military families. Full-time military members move frequently and usually live far from their civilian friends and family members. It is important to reach out to other military families for friendship and support. Guard members, on the other hand, choose where they live and are able to put down roots. We have close ties to our chosen communities. Because of this, other Guard families may not factor into our social circle. We all have limited free time and it is hard enough just keeping up with our family members, co-workers, and our circle of friends. On top of everything else, we must work our schedules around drill weekends, training, and deployments. It is no wonder that we feel stretched.

Of course, participating in Guard social functions isn't mandatory. In my opinion, family members should not be judged if they choose not to participate in extra activities. If you support your Soldier's Guard career and take care of yourself while he or she is fulfilling their duty, you are doing enough. Actually, you are doing more than enough. Soldiers who are happy at home and encouraged by family members have an advantage over those who go it alone.

But just as it is with civilian careers, it is always a good idea to get to know your co-workers. It gives you insight into your Soldier's job and being able to match a name to a face gives you a useful frame of reference. Attending events will help your Soldier and it will help you too. In the civilian workplace, a charming and well-rounded spouse goes a long way. Jon has helped me make friends (and disarm cnemics) at many work functions. I try to do the same for him by attending Guard events and socializing with his Guard friends and co-workers.

From Worst to First

Before I became actively engaged with the Guard family, I felt very disconnected from the Guard part of my husband's life. It was an important part of his life but was a big mystery to me. Quite frankly, I resented it. Many times, I felt like he was choosing the Guard over me. Our life seemed to operate around drill weekends. We had just finished one drill weekend and BAM it was time for another. I really think there should be a special calendar just for Guard families because the weeks fly by when your Soldier is home "(didn't you just have drill?)" and drag on when they are deployed. Guard social life makes me feel like I am a part of the Guard too. The social events that used to feel like an obligation are now something I look forward to. I remember taking an early flight out of New York so that I could make it back in time for a Guard dinner. I had every excuse not to attend, but I didn't want to miss an opportunity to see my friends and relax with Jon in such a special setting. The more you participate, the more comfortable you will feel. I always look forward to events and I am sad if we are not able to attend. I think the same thing will happen to you. The fact that you are reading this book means that you are interested in knowing more about Guard life. Guard events are the perfect place to show off your new-found knowledge.

Networking

From a professional perspective, Guard events offer a chance to network. A Guardsman is a real life Clark Kent/Superman: businessman, teacher, policewoman, veterinarian, dentist by day and Soldier by night. Or something like that!

Even if their military dossier means nothing to you, don't forget that they may have some worthwhile connections that *are* of interest to you. Need a good accountant? Start asking around. Thinking about selling your home? Here is an opportunity to find a trustworthy real estate agent. Guard spouses are also a treasure trove for networking and inspiration. In addition to professional networking, you will meet people who are ready and willing to help you out with any conceivable need that you may have. Need a new truck? Start asking around and you will definitely meet somebody in the Guard who owns a dealership or works for one. Want to start a business on eBay® and not sure where to start? You will find somebody who is already doing it and is happy to share what they know. The Guard family is a small, close-knit community and takes care of its own. If you need something and don't know where to start, start with your friends in the Guard.

Membership Has Its Privileges

My favorite reason for participating in Guard social life is because it is exclusive. You don't have to pay $25,000 a year to belong to a country club so you can put on a sequined dress once a year and attend a silent auction. You are part of a truly exclusive club. This club is so exclusive that no amount of money can buy you a membership. And membership has its privileges. Anybody can go out for dinner and a movie. But only a select few are invited to attend a military ball. Most people only get to wear a formal gown or tuxedo if they are lucky enough to go on a cruise or unlucky enough to be in yet another bridal party; National Guard members have many opportunities to step out in their finest. How many people get to attend a Dining Out or see uniformed mixers concoct a vat of punch that even a bartender at TGI Fridays could not duplicate? Not many. You are one of the lucky ones. It is true that life in the Guard can be difficult and inconvenient, but it can also be fun and uplifting.

When I worked as a marketing professional, the firm I worked for paid for my membership to a very hoity-toity private women's club. It was a great chance to rub elbows with the local movers and shakers. I was one of the youngest members at the club and it was always a challenge to make conversation with other members and their spouses. When I met Jon, I was relieved to have a wingman to drag to events. I am a total introvert and could go for months without talking to anybody. Jon is much more outgoing and can make conversation with a wall. The first event we attended as a couple was the club's annual holiday ball. Jon decided to forgo the tuxedo that I made him buy in favor of his Dress Blues. I wasn't sure what I thought of the idea but when he told me that his Blues were the equivalent of wearing a penguin suit, I backed off. At the time, his Guard life was still a bit of a mystery to me and I wasn't prepared for the reaction we received when we walked into the room. Basically, even though the room was filled with all kinds of interesting people, all eyes were on us (really, on him). As I looked around the room at all the elegantly clad men in tuxedos and women in formal gowns, I realized that all the money in the world could not buy the honor of wearing the uniform. You earn the right to wear it. It was a magical moment and very humbling. I knew how lucky I was to have a Soldier in my life. Within minutes, we were surrounded by veterans of all ages sharing their stories and memories. After two years of struggling to connect with the club's membership, I had happened upon an unexpected but powerful connection. I met more people that night than I had met in the three years prior. And they never forgot me after that night. The magic of the military!

Military Etiquette and Protocol

In the civilian world, the rules are pretty clear. We have all attended enough business functions, birthday parties, and weddings to get the basic formula of what we do, what we say, and how we behave. But the military is a bit more complicated. In addition to battling the basic etiquette challenges that we all endure from time-to-time (remembering names, which fork to use, etc.), we have other issues to deal with like flag etiquette and receiving lines. The good news is that good manners are universal. If you are polite, pleasant, and in control: you have nothing to worry about. Certainly, there is a learning curve with military social life but learning is part of the process and part of the fun.

The first time I attended a formal Dining Out, I was overwhelmed. Who wouldn't be? I had barely taken a sip from my cocktail when I was whisked through a receiving line of "important people" (I know this now but back then I didn't know who they were!). I clutched onto my vodka sour as if my life depended on it, not knowing that bringing food and drinks through a receiving line is verboten. After I stuttered my way (one-handed) through the receiving line, I entered the dining room. I didn't know when to sit, when to stand, or what to say. Thank goodness for my street smarts. With laser-like precision, I quickly identified the classiest looking woman in the room and followed her lead. If she clapped, I clapped. If she toasted, I toasted. If she stood, I stood. Considering that I was a novice, it was a respectable performance. The only problem was that I was so worried about doing everything right that I didn't enjoy the great program and great company. That, in itself, is the ultimate breech of etiquette. Even though I survived the evening, I decided it might be a good idea to educate myself on the basics of military etiquette and protocol so I would be more comfortable at the next event. I bought a copy of *Service Etiquette* (4th Edition), by Oretha Swartz. This is the holy grail of military protocol and etiquette. In addition, after searching online I came across reams of information with advice for situations that (thankfully) most of us will never have to deal with. Entertaining the King of Sudan? Do this. Planning a cocktail party for foreign dignitaries? Do this. Meeting your Congressman for cocktails? Do this. Serving as the Grand Marshal in a parade? Do this. Toasting a retiring General? Say this. Kid having a tantrum in the middle of TJ Maxx? Still haven't found the chapter on that.

But everything else is covered in detail. I highly recommend adding this book to your personal library. Ask your Soldier to pick up a copy for you the next time they visit the base bookstore or order it through Amazon. It is a great go-to book not only in your military life, but your civilian life as well.

In addition to my copy of *Service Etiquette*, I collect vintage military etiquette books. I love the "Mad Men" era rules and regulations and—if you can find them—these little gems make great gifts for your Guard girlfriends. They will enjoy reading about the days when women wore white gloves and hats to teas and carried formal calling cards. Back then, newly-arrived Officers were expected to call on their commanders at their homes as a courtesy. It was like a constant Open House!

Things are much different now. The Grand Baroque tea service and cucumber sandwiches have been replaced with a pitcher of margaritas and a basket of chips. And if you show up at my house unannounced, a nanosecond after the dog sounds his warning bark, I grab the kids, close the blinds, and hide in my master bedroom closet (see introvert above). Needless to say, I don't think that I would have done well back in the day. It is good that things are not nearly as complicated as they used to be. If you are really lucky, the Guard people in your state organization have already done the work for you. The Arizona National Guard Family Programs Office went through reams of information and put together a wonderful, concise document that provides an "everything you need to know and nothing more" view of customs, courtesies, protocol, and etiquette. The California National Guard has a Protocol Officer on staff. There are also official documents available online that will help you find detailed information on etiquette:

- Google "PAM 600-60" and you will find "A Guide to Protocol and Etiquette for Official Entertainment."
- Google "PAM 600-15" and you will find everything you need to know about a traditional Dining In/Dining Out.

Even though many military customs have gone by the wayside, I would highly recommend a quick review of some of the excellent resources available through the military or at your local library or bookstore. Understanding the roots of military etiquette will give you an appreciation and respect for the traditions that have withstood the test of time. You will quickly realize how lucky you are to experience military customs first hand.

What to Wear?

This is always THE question! If only Stacy London were available to provide personal consultations for all of us. Before I go into details about different types of military events, let me answer the first question that passes through many minds when they are invited to a party, "What am I supposed to wear?"

In the business casual world that we live where hip-hugging sweatpants that have "Juicy" written across the rear end are commonplace at Sunday church services, the formal event is almost non-existent. It seems that people don't like to dress up. I really don't get this. Sure, I like to be comfortable when I am at home or running errands, but I also love to dress up and go out on the town from time-to-time.

The military is a very traditional establishment and one of the best things about having a Soldier in your life is being able to dress up for formal events. There is nothing like basking in the stardust of a Soldier wearing their Dress Blues or Mess Blues. For those of us who were not invited to our senior prom, it is the ultimate revenge. Take advantage of your chance to walk the red carpet by dressing appropriately.

Formal Versus Informal

Even though you will see invitations that use terms such as business casual, there are only two types of events: formal or informal. Events such as a military ball, Dining Out, or banquet are formal events. Events such as change-of-command ceremonies, Family Day at the armory, company or battalion picnics, or theme events (luau, western, etc.) are informal events. Just how formal or informal they are is open for interpretation. The easiest way to determine the correct categorization is by looking at what your Soldier is told to wear.

That's right. You don't have to worry about dressing your Soldier, they will know exactly what to wear because military invitations will clearly state the required uniform for military personnel. And what a relief that is!

If a Soldier is told to wear Dress Blues or Mess Blues, it is a formal event. If he or she does not own Blues they will wear their Class A (remember, uniforms are changing) uniform with a white shirt and black bowtie. Invitations may give the option of a civilian equivalent and some Soldiers may opt for a nice suit or tuxedo/cocktail dress or gown, but 99% of Soldiers will be in uniform. When your Soldier is dressed formally, you will also dress formally.

This means that civilian men should wear a tuxedo or their nicest suit and tie. Of course, things are not quite as simple for women, but there are a variety of options for every type of taste and style:

- A long dress in either a ball gown or sheath style.
- A tea-length or knee-length cocktail dress made of evening fabric or containing evening embellishments. If you wear a shorter dress, make sure to formalize it with accessories i.e., beautiful shoes, jewelry, fancy hand bag, wrap, etc.
- A beautiful skirted evening suit made of formal fabric such as brocade or silk. It may include details such as jeweled buttons. This isn't a suit you would wear to a business meeting but a suit you would wear to an evening wedding.
- Dressy separates such as a long or tea-length skirt or silk palazzo pants paired with a beautiful blouse, jeweled sweater, or dressy shell. If you are going for separates, fabric is the key. There is a big difference between a silk or chiffon blouse and a cotton blouse. Anything bejeweled or sequined is perfect.

Formal affairs require formal attire. You should look like you are going somewhere special. Many women go all out and wear long dresses to every formal event. I love this and applaud formality but I am much more comfortable wearing a shorter cocktail dress. Either option is acceptable for most formal military events. However, if you are invited to a special ball at the governor's mansion or to a banquet at a national professional organization, go all out and wear a full-length evening gown.

In the civilian world, it is wise to invest in a few classic pieces that you can wear frequently over the years. But in the military, you will see the same faces over and over again. Depending on how many events you attend a year (we typically attend anywhere from one to four events), you may not want to wear the same dress to every event. I check in with my husband at the beginning of the year to get an idea of what type of events he anticipates. I am a bargain hunter and don't like to spend a lot on formalwear. There are great deals available on formal dresses and accessories at department stores and discount chains all the time. If you shop off-season, you will find beautiful dresses on the clearance racks. Even if I don't have an event on the calendar, if I find a nice, classic cocktail dress at a great price, I buy it and stash it away. Shopping ahead gives you time to get alterations and find the right accessories. If you wait until the last minute, the pressure is on and you may end up spending more than you have to or settling for something that you are not entirely happy with. I would also advise checking out your local upscale consignment shops. I recently purchased an incredible summer cocktail dress with the tags still on it for $30 (and the gold sandals to match it). After I've worn a formal dress, unless I absolutely know that I will wear it again, I dry clean it and bring it back to the store to consign.

And one last tip, invest in something to wear over your gown or cocktail dress, a velvet or satin coat or a pretty wool shawl. You don't want to be standing outside shivering at a winter event. Or worse yet, be forced to wear your puffer coat over your ensemble.

Invitations to informal events will instruct your Soldier exactly how they are to dress. If no uniform is stated, assume that they will wear their uniform of the day which is usually the ACU. Sometimes military events are labeled as business casual or some other term that leaves a lot of room for interpretation. This means the event is informal. But just because an event is informal, does not mean you should wear jeans or shorts. Informal means that the event isn't formal. It does not mean that you shouldn't look nice.

If the Guardsman in your life happens to be male, never rely on his opinion regarding what *you* should wear. He may be able to hit a target from a mile away and run a complicated mission with his eyes closed, but I can promise you that he isn't as adept at choosing the right ensemble for you. If my husband had his way, I would be wearing a box-pleated ball gown to a barbeque. Some of my girlfriend's husbands are just the opposite and will purposely downplay an event to avoid investing in a new formal dress. I will never forget when my husband was company commander and we had the honor of meeting all of the Soldier's family members at the holiday party. The event was held in the armory on a Sunday afternoon and it was informal. But there were no invitations issued and it was up to the Soldiers to communicate the details to their spouses. That's a disaster waiting to happen if you ask me.

One poor woman was in a long, formal dress and when she came through the receiving line, I knew she was uncomfortable. I said to her, "You look beautiful. Don't even worry about it." She rolled her eyes, pointed to her husband, and we both just laughed. We both knew that she was going to have his head on a platter the minute she got him alone. Who could blame her?

Your Soldier's job is to make sure his own uniform is ready to go. Your job is to follow the guidelines provided in this book so you are always dressed appropriately. And dressing appropriately does not mean that you need a new wardrobe or should spend more than you can afford. I find cute things at TJ Maxx and Target all the time. I also borrow clothes from my sisters and friends if I don't have extra money to spend on a new outfit. I have a good friend with plenty of money who buys amazing designer clothes at consignment stores and on eBay®. There are a lot of ways to look great on a budget.

My goal is to always fall somewhere in the middle of the formality spectrum. I don't want to be the dressiest person in the room and I don't want to be the most casual person in the room. When I am invited to an informal event in the military, I think to myself, "Dry clean only." You don't have to take this literally. What it means is to wear something crisp and clean. For men, there is a big difference between a nice, pressed golf shirt and one that has been washed 500 times. For women, there is a big difference between a nice pair of slacks and the cargo pants that you wear to the grocery store. Err on the side of being overdressed, which means no jeans, shorts, message-t-shirts, or tennis shoes. If you are invited to an informal daytime event, such as a change-of-command ceremony or reception, wear what you would wear to a nice restaurant for lunch. For women, a nice pair of slacks paired with a blouse or sweater is perfect. In the summer months, a skirt, sundress, or dressy Capri pants with a pretty top is a good choice. For men, try a nice pair of chinos with a button-down shirt or a nice, pressed short-sleeved shirt. A golf shirt is fine, but it should be pressed and in good shape (nothing shabby). If the event is in the evening, step it up a notch. Women can add dressy accessories and shoes. Men can add a sport coat sans tie.

I know, I know—who wears a sport coat? A smart man does! If you ever attend a non-uniformed event with military people, you will notice that most of the high-ranking male officers wear jackets. Discerning gentlemen know that a sport coat is a wise strategy for informal occasions when the dress code is blurry. They know that if other men are wearing golf shirts, they can lose their jacket. But if other men are wearing suits, they are going to be in the zone. Make sure that your husband isn't one of those insecure smart alecks who say something like, "Why are you so dressed up?" to a man who has the good taste to wear a sport coat to an informal event. He should worry about his own clothes and not make passive aggressive comments on what other people are wearing. A more appropriate response is to say "You look sharp," and wear a sport coat next time. You can pick up sport coats at reasonable prices year round.

If the event is informal but clearly something casual (i.e., a picnic, parade, child-centered event), feel free to wear something comfortable. But comfortable does not mean something that you would walk the dog in. Wear something that you would wear to a movie. For women, a nice pair of jeans, shorts, khakis, or Capri pants is a good choice. For men, nice jeans, chinos, cargo pants, or shorts will work. Please leave the frayed hems, cut-offs, faded denim and athletic wear at home. Ask yourself, "If I ran into an old girlfriend or boyfriend, would I be embarrassed?" If your answer is "yes," it's time to change.

No matter what type of event you are attending, don't wear anything that is too revealing. All of your stuff needs to be in its place. You can be sexy without a peep show. The backless dress or exposed midriff that worked on New Year's Eve will not be appropriate at a Guard event. Nobody wants to see any piercings or tattoos, either. Remember, the military is a conservative organization and being a Soldier is a profession. You are mingling with your Soldier's co-workers and should keep this in mind when choosing the right outfit.

A Typical Formal Event

Every military affair is different. Depending on what the occasion is, some features may be added or removed. Some events include speakers, some don't. Some include dancing after dinner, some don't. The invitation will give you an idea of what to expect as far as the program goes. If not, don't worry about it. Every event that I have ever attended includes a program. You will find this at your place setting or on your chair and it will tell you everything you need to know about the order of events.

Traditionally, formal invitations to Dining Outs or formal banquets were engraved or handwritten. But technology and practicality make it more likely that today's invitations will be a simple flyer-style via e-mail. Either way, you should RSVP as soon as possible and send your check to the appropriate person. A typical formal event will cost $25-$60 per person. Rates will be pro-rated based on your Soldier's rank which means that the higher your rank, the more you pay. The people who plan these events do a great job of negotiating the best possible rates. Many events are held in hotels and sometimes you will have the option of booking a room at a reduced military rate. If you are planning on having a drink or two at the event, consider making a night of it. Information about the hotel and the negotiated rate will be provided with your invitation. You are responsible for reserving and paying for your own room. Do this as quickly as possible and make sure you meet any deadlines given. If you wait, you will end up paying significantly more for your room or the hotel will fill up and you will have to find other accommodations.

Formal events are often part of a larger program. Soldiers may attend official training or educational events the day of the event. If this is the case, your Soldier will be on orders and will be reimbursed for travel and lodging expenses. But this isn't always the case so make sure you know what the parameters are in advance.

Social Hour

Many formal events are held at hotels or conference centers. The set up is similar to that of a wedding. Typically, the Guard party will have its own area for happy hour as well as a large banquet room for a seated dinner. Arrive on time so you can have a chance to socialize and get in the spirit of things before the official program begins. This is the time to greet your friends and meet new people. At some formal events, the cost of your meal may include drink tickets or wine provided at each table, but typically you will purchase your drinks at a cash bar. Even if drink tickets are issued, be sure to remember to bring cash to tip the bartenders.

Sometimes the sponsoring organization will set up a hospitality room in a meeting, conference, or larger suite room within the hotel where attendees can have complimentary drinks and simple munchies (these may be underwritten by a corporate sponsor). There may be a host in the room or a team of Soldiers serving as bartenders (again: always tip the bartenders—even if you know them!). Or, it may be a serve yourself program. Feel free to grab a drink and mingle with people in the hospitality room, but don't hideaway for too long. Take your drink and join the party.

It goes without saying that you should never drink more than you can handle at an official Guard function. Fortunately, there will be enough going on to keep your interest whether you are drinking or not. If you do choose to drink and you are not spending the night on site, make sure you designate a driver or make arrangements for a cab. I have found that we are so rushed on the days of Guard events that I barely have time to eat. Between coordinating with the babysitter, getting the kids settled, and getting dressed, I am frazzled and hungry by the time I finally get in the car. And the night has just begun. Be warned, formal military events are not fast affairs and it takes a while to actually get to the dinner portion of the program. There are usually a lot of people at these events and you may be watching the head table start in on their desserts before you have set eyes on your entrée. Sometimes I am so wound up at these types of events that I pick at my food and don't get enough to eat. Plan accordingly! Have a light snack before you leave the house or do what we do—stop at a drive through and have a hamburger on the way to the event.

The Receiving Line

Happy hour ends with the announcement that the receiving line has begun. In the Army, it is ladies first; the lady precedes the man in the receiving line. Typically, thirty minutes are set aside for the receiving line. Be punctual and get in line when the request is made to do so. The first person in line will be an aide or announcer. You will tell them your name and they will pass this information to the next person in the receiving line. You don't shake hands with the announcer/aide but if you forget this little rule, don't worry about it. It isn't a big deal. Ideally, your name will travel down the line and you will not have to repeat it over and over again. If not, just quietly introduce yourself and shake hands with everybody in the receiving line. The key is to keep moving. You only have to go through the line once but the people that you are meeting have to meet hundreds of people. They also have to keep the event running on schedule and in the military, punctuality is a big deal. Thus, the receiving line is a simple formality and isn't the time to make conversation or discuss your latest news. If your Soldier is of the chatty persuasion, gently remind him or her before the receiving line to stay close to you and move through the line quickly. There should be absolutely no shop talk or career talk. Just say, "Hello, nice to meet you," or "Nice to see you again," and move on.

Pre-Dinner

After the receiving line, you will enter the dining room. When you enter the dining area, find your table quickly. It is likely that tables will be pre-designated for certain groups or units. If there is a seating chart, it will be displayed in a prominent location. Sometimes, you are asked to write your name on the seating chart. Whatever you do, don't start switching tables around or complain that you are not near your friends. If, for some reason, it isn't clear where you are to sit or somebody is sitting in your spot, quietly find another place to sit. Don't ask to trade seats with other people so you can sit where you want to sit (my pet peeve on airplanes). And whatever you do, don't save your seat by leaning the chair against the table. The best way to save your seat is to stand behind your seat and wait for the program to begin.

When your table mates arrive at the table, introduce yourself to the people you don't know. After introductions are made, you should stand behind your chair (but don't hold on to it or lean on it) and wait for the program to start. The reason that you don't take your seat is because more often than not there is a flag line or the head table will walk into the room together. This requires that you stand. If other people are in their seats versus standing behind them (been there, done that), just stand behind your chair and act casually. They will stand up eventually.

Those assigned to the head table will enter the dining room last. The flag line is centered behind the head table. (Sometimes it is centered behind the receiving line and moved into the dining room.) Flags are arranged in the order of precedence. The United States flag gets top billing and is located in the place of honor. If flags are grouped, then Old Glory is in the center of the grouping and at the highest point of the group. If appropriate, "Ruffles and Flourishes" will sound as those seated at the head table enter the room. After they arrive (you, your Soldier, and the rest of the assembly are standing behind your chairs), a Color Guard marches into the room and posts the colors. After that, the National Anthem may be played. During the National Anthem, your Soldier will stand at attention and you will hold your hand over your heart.

After the Color Guard has left the room, the president asks the chaplain or another appropriate person to deliver the invocation. At a Dining Out, the president of the mess will propose a toast to the president of the United States followed by toasts made by Mister or Madame Vice, but we will discuss how that works later.

When you sit down, take a deep breath and check out the program provided. It is time to relax and enjoy the rest of the evening.

The Dinner

Now is my favorite part of the night—recess! To truly enjoy yourself, I would suggest reviewing some of the basic rules of table manners before attending a big event. Review your copy of *Service Etiquette* or look online. You will be reminded of basics such as where to put your fork and knife when you are finished with your meal, where to put your napkin if you have to use the restroom during dinner, as well as often forgotten rules such as always passing the salt and pepper as a pair (even if a person only requests one) and buttering your bread or roll in pieces as you eat, versus swiping the whole thing at once.

When you first sit down, the first dilemma that you will be confronted with immediately is making sure you know where, exactly, your place setting is and making sure you don't grab somebody else's water goblet. If you need a reminder, check online or in the back of your Betty Crocker cookbook. I have been to a lot of formal dinners over the years. But no matter how much I think I know there is always a flash of panic when I try to get my bearings. The problem is that all of the graphics show one simple place setting. What they should show is how confusing things get when there are ten place settings crammed on a single round table. Talk about chaos. Here is a tip that will save you every time: remember the three letters BMW—bread, meal, water. Your bread (B) plate is on your left, your dinner (M) plate is in the middle, and your water (W) is on the right. The following illustrations show an informal place setting and a formal place setting. At a typical Guard event, you will be presented with a "hybrid" of both of these. You may not have all the specialty silverware as you would at a true formal table, but you

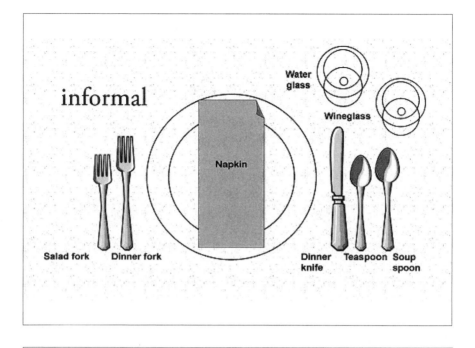

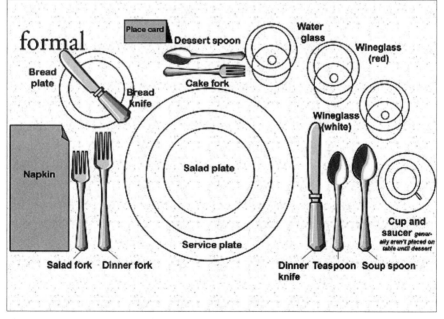

will have a bread plate. Either way, if you remember "BMW" you will be able to get acclimated.

After you have taken your seat and smiled at your tablemates (you may have already introduced yourselves while you were standing behind your seats), it is time to eat and make dinner conversation. Before you launch into conversation, give everybody a moment to get comfortable. Many times, your salad will already be in place as well as rolls, butter, and a non-alcoholic beverage such as iced tea. After the head table begins eating, you can start on your salad course. Be sure to offer to pass dressings, rolls, butter, and other communal items. If you were given a meal choice in advance, you will either be provided with some type of designation (such as a colored piece of paper) that alerts the wait staff to your preference. Or, they will simply ask you what you ordered. This may be easier said than done at a large event.

As far as making conversation, we all want excellent dinner conversation but sometimes there is so much noise in the room that we can't have a conversation that includes all ten people at the table. Don't use this as an excuse to only talk to your date. Talk to the person next to you and do the best you can to talk to as many people as possible. But if you have to yell to be heard or speak loudly to talk to people across the table, don't do it. Just make sure that you talk to them after the dinner program has ended.

It is worth noting that you may be seated with civilians who are not familiar with the National Guard or our protocols. At a recent state Family Readiness conference, I was surprised to find out that all of our table mates were civilian volunteers who were being honored at the event. If this is the case, avoid talking shop and do your best to facilitate a conversation that everybody can participate in.

The Speaker

If there is a speaker, they will usually speak during dessert. Remember, it is the speaker, not your cheesecake, which should be the center of your attention. And if you are one of the last tables to be served, you may still be working on your entrée. It is fine to eat during the program. But do it quietly. Don't clank your glass or scrape your silverware against your plate. If you can't eat without clanking, then don't eat until the speaker is finished.

It is likely that the staff will be clearing tables during the speaker portion of the program and this can be very distracting. The people in charge of the event should be wary of this and make sure the staff are instructed to clear quietly, or wait until the end of the program altogether.

By all means, stop talking when the speaker is announced and look in their direction. Even if you are still eating, give them your attention. If you are finished with your meal and your back is to the speaker, it is perfectly

Top 10 Etiquette Tips

- Once seated, unfold your napkin and place it on your lap. Don't shake it open. If you excuse yourself from the table, loosely fold your napkin and place it to the left or right of your plate. Never place your napkin on your chair. At the end of dinner, leave the napkin tidily on the place setting. Don't wad it up or refold it.
- While eating, rest the knife and fork on either side of the plate between mouthfuls. When you have finished eating, place them side by side in the center of the plate.
- Forks should not be turned over unless being used for eating peas, sweet corn kernels, rice, or other similar foods. Don't "fist" your utensils.
- Don't use your bread for dipping into soups or mopping up sauces.
- Loud eating noises such as slurping and burping are very impolite. Don't slurp you coffee or soup! If it's too hot, wait until it cools.
- Don't stretch across the table crossing other guests to reach food, wine, or condiments. Instead ask a guest sitting close to pass the item to you. Pass items to the right (counterclockwise) with each dinner guest helping himself. However, if someone sitting to your immediate left requests something, don't send the dish all the way around the table. It's perfectly fine to directly pass the dish to the left.
- Pass the salt and pepper shaker together. Don't separate them.
- When eating meat, always cut and eat one small piece at a time. If you are eating American style, you may put your knife down, switch your fork to your other hand and eat your bite. If you are eating continental style, you may cut the piece of meat and eat it without setting your knife on your plate.
- When bread or a roll are served on a bread/butter plate, break the bread with your fingers into pieces small enough for one or two bites; butter a pulled apart piece and then eat it. Don't butter the entire roll or piece of bread at one time.
- Don't forget to make polite conversation with those guests around you. If the event is loud, try and make conversation with the people sitting directly next to you. Foodies note: conversation shouldn't center around the food. It is best not to comment on the food—either negatively or positively.

acceptable to gently turn your chair in their direction and give them your full attention. If people at your table are talking while the speaker is talking, say nothing. It isn't your job to "sshhh" them (or other people at the table), but you should not engage in the conversation at all. If your Soldier is talking while the speaker is talking, give them "the look" or a quick kick under the table. That should do the trick.

I have to say that I am always a little surprised by people's behavior during a speech. Many people treat this time as free time rather than an important part of the program. They are so engrossed with their dessert that they barely look up from their plate. There is no need for this. You have the rest of the night to finish your dessert and nobody is going to take it away from you until you want them to. Or, they are antsy and want to talk to their friends. But there is time for that later. This is a formal part of the program and requires your respect and attention.

The Dining In/Dining Out

The military banquet and Dining Out share many things in common. Both are formal events and are an opportunity to dress in your finest. Both are sit-down affairs that are typically held at hotels or conference centers, sometimes in conjunction with official Army training or educational programs. Each typically includes a social hour, receiving line, dinner, and a guest speaker. Sometimes the evening includes after-dinner dancing. The biggest difference between a banquet and Dining Out is that a banquet will have a more civilian tone, similar to a professional event or a large party such as a groom's dinner. A Dining Out, on the other hand, is a formal military event shaped by tradition. Only people in or closely associated with the military will ever have the opportunity to attend a Dining Out. It is a very special event.

Perhaps you have heard of the Dining Out's sister affair, the Dining In? You will not have to worry about attending a Dining In because, to put it bluntly, you will not be invited. Dining Ins are solely for military personnel and very select civilian guests and honorees. The Dining In will include the same content as a Dining Out but things will get a lot more, how shall I say it, wild. If your Soldier attends a Dining In, don't be upset that you are not invited. A Dining In is like a Dean Martin celebrity roast times ten. Everybody is a candidate for the hot seat and a thick skin is required. You are much better off in the comfort and safety of your own home.

The purpose of both a Dining In and Dining Out is to boost morale and camaraderie and recognize individual or unit achievements. A Dining Out is an elegant affair that includes spouses, dates, and other guests. It is a chance to mix and mingle with other Soldiers and their spouses. This is a very special occasion and you should definitely attend any Dining Outs that you are invited to. But just because a Dining Out is more refined than a Dining In, does not mean it isn't an adventure. Parts of the program are deep and meaningful and parts of the program are downright silly. And the best part of a Dining Out is the presence of a unique character known as The Vice.

The Vice

You may first notice Mr. or Madame Vice when they call members and guests to the dining room. The Vice is selected for his or her wit and ability to think on their feet. When you enter the dining room at a Dining Out, you will notice a small table set for one. This isn't the dunce's corner; it is where Mr. or Madame Vice sits. The Vice sits alone and works very hard to make the evening fun and keep things moving along. The Vice does not have a script but has the ability to speak extraneously. Throughout the evening, the Vice will deliver toasts, make jokes, and keep the program on schedule. (Helpful hint: if you are shy and don't like to be in the spotlight, it is best that you and your date not mess with the Vice.)

The following represents an ideal flow of events at a Dining In or Dining Out. This is only a sample of procedures and is sometimes altered slightly. However, most groups stick as closely to the traditional program as possible because that's what makes it meaningful.

- Lounge opens for refreshments. Guests arrive. Host Officer meets and greets guests. Receiving line (optional).
- Mess call. Mr./Madam Vice rings dinner chimes and group assembles in dining room. All remain standing behind their chairs.
- The mess is formally opened by the president with one rap of the gavel.
- Posting of the colors.
- Invocation by chaplain or other.
- Toasts.
- President seats the mess.
- Welcoming remarks.

- Head table introduced.
- Toast by Mr. Vice: "To our guests." Members (Soldiers) stand. Guests remain seated. Response is "Hear hear."
- President invites members of the mess to be seated. President: "Mr. Vice, test the meal to ensure it is edible." Mr. Vice: (samples the meal) "Ladies and Gentlemen, this meal is fit for human consumption." The salad and main course are served. Music may begin.
- The president may call for a break (two raps of the gavel). If so, return to the mess when directed and remain standing. The president will seat the mess (one rap of the gavel).
- Dessert and coffee are served.
- Individual achievements/awards presented.
- Introduction of guest speaker by the president.
- Address by guest speaker President: "Mr. Vice?" Mr. Vice: "Yes, Mr. President?" President: "A toast to our distinguished speaker." (Members rise) Mr. Vice: (Appropriate toast ending with), "To our distinguished speaker . . . " Response: "Hear, hear."
- Closing remarks from the president.
- Retire the colors.
- President adjourns the mess (two raps of the gavel).
- President announces entertainment. Turns program over to the master of ceremonies. Entertainment/informal circulating begin.
- Proceedings are closed when the unit flag is cased or when the president announces conclusion of the program. Members remain until the guest of honor has departed or when properly excused.

The Punch Ceremony

A Dining Out may also include a Punch Ceremony. At a unit Dining In, protocol dictates that this be held before the dinner in a separate room from the dining room. At a Dining Out, the Punch Ceremony may be done in the dining room at a time that works best with the schedule and program. The Punch Ceremony is entertaining and is conducted in a very particular way. Luckily, you don't have to memorize a script or do anything for the ceremony but listen and enjoy it. The purpose is to read the unit's lineage while mixing together a concoction that tells a story. The Master of Ceremonies or host will serve as the narrator for the ceremony. He or she will be assisted by the Master of Punch who oversees the mixers and any other assistants involved. The Master of Punch will present each bottle of spirits (and other ingredients, but I will not ruin the surprise for you) to the presiding Officer for approval before they are added to the punch mixture. A junior Officer or the Vice will serve as a guinea pig and test the punch. After it is deemed acceptable, the Master of Punch presents the first cup to the presiding Officer for his approval. Upon approval, the punch is distributed to the rest of the assembly. Depending on the size of the assembly, there may be one central punch bowl or several punch stations around the room. Proceed to the punch bowl to get your punch. After all members have filled their cups and returned to their tables, a toast will be proposed:

> *"A toast to our heritage and comrades who have gone before us. May we serve our country and our unit in honor."*

Response by the mess members is:

> *"To (unit designation)!"*

If the ceremony is held before the dinner in an adjacent room, Mr. Vice will ask for the assembly to leave their punch glasses in the cocktail room and proceed to the dining room. As discussed earlier, you will stand behind your chair and wait for the official party/head table to arrive.

The Military Wedding

There is no such thing as a military wedding service. Wedding ceremonies are usually religious ceremonies. What makes a civilian wedding a "military" wedding is the attire and incorporation of traditions that are distinct to the service.

Weddings held on military installations or at service academy chapels will definitely feel very military in nature, particularly because many of the guests will be service members. In this instance, there are particular formalities involved with invitations and seating arrangements. A National Guardsman's wedding will cater toward civilian guests and, even if other Guardsmen are invited to attend, there is no need to get caught up in military protocol. Rely on your wedding planning book to guide you through the process and you will be fine. If you need help addressing invitations to members of the military, refer to your copy of *Service Etiquette*.

Just because there is no such thing as an official military wedding, does not mean that you can't have what others will consider a military wedding. Here are some suggestions:

- Dress the military member in uniform versus a tuxedo or suit.
- Have members of the Guard serve as ushers and execute the arch of sabers (this is for commissioned service members only). These Soldiers will also be in uniform.
- Cut the cake with the groom's saber.
- Incorporate military-inspired touches into the ceremony and reception.

Can I get Married in a Military Chapel by a Military Chaplain?

You can be married in a military chapel; most major Guard installations have a chapel. However, in these post-9/11 days, getting on post is difficult for civilians. If you don't have the appropriate sticker on your car, it can be an ordeal. Anyone thinking of getting married on a military installation must carefully consider the bureaucratic ins and outs of getting their wedding guests onto the installation. If you are interested in having a Guard Chaplain perform your wedding ceremony, you will have to consult with the Chaplain directly. Just keep in mind that regular Army chaplains are full-time employees who are paid a full-time salary. Guard chaplains are mostly on drill status. Weddings are involved events typically held over the weekend. Like every other Guardsman, a chaplain has already committed at least one weekend a month to the Army. Please take this into consideration. Even if you want to pay the chaplain for his time, this is prohibited. If you do have a chaplain perform your ceremony, he or she may wear Dress Blues or whatever the ministerial robes are of his or her denomination. If you want your military chaplain to wear Dress Blues, be sure to ask beforehand. Chaplains can officiate in a civilian church. Military custom dictates that you extend a formal invitation to the reception to the chaplain and his or her spouse.

Attire

Remember, your ceremony should cater toward your civilian guests. Thus, there is no need to include any type of uniform instruction on your wedding invitation. To do this would confuse people. Your ushers will know that they are to wear uniforms. If other Guard members are invited guests, you may ask them to come in uniform, although you can't dictate. It is likely they will ask other invited guests if they are coming in uniform, so have your Soldier pass the word.

Both Officers and enlisted personnel will wear the uniform that's appropriate for the formality of the occasion and season. For Officers, dinner or Mess Dress uniform is in accordance with black tie. For Noncommissioned Officers and enlisted men, Dress Blues or Army Green uniforms are appropriate for both formal and informal weddings. If the bride is an Officer, she may wear a traditional bridal gown or her uniform. A boutonniere is never worn with uniform.

The Arch of Sabers

When I was planning my wedding, I remember reading an article in a bridal magazine that offered creative ideas for civilians who wanted to incorporate the tradition of a saber arch into their wedding. There was actually a photograph of a yuppie couple walking underneath an arch of golf clubs. I mean, please. Is nothing sacred? The arch of sabers is a great military tradition and, unlike an arch of polo sticks, actually symbolizes something important: the military's welcome and the couple's safe transition into their new life together. In the Army, only commissioned servicemen and servicewomen may participate in the arch of swords or sabers. It is ideal that six ushers in uniform perform this ceremony, but more may participate. Ushers may be in uniform of one or more services. Rifles can be substituted for the sabers if there is difficulty in obtaining the needed amount. It is up to the military member (whether bride or groom) to oversee and coordinate this effort. They are responsible for locating the sabers, communicating with the ushers, and making sure that the group is well-rehearsed. Ushers should be included in the wedding rehearsal and be invited to the rehearsal dinner. If this isn't possible, your Soldier should meet them at the church well before the guests arrive to go over the logistics.

The arch of sabers takes place immediately following the ceremony, preferably when the couple leaves the chapel or church. The ushers will march down the aisle at the end of the ceremony and lead the couple out of the church. They will form an arch for the couple to walk under. Traditionally, this is done on the front steps or walk of the church. If logistics or weather is a factor, the arch may be formed inside the chapel or church. Many couples have two arches of sabers, one in the church and one outside. If you want to do the arch of sabers indoors, be sure to get permission from your pastor or priest to do so and communicate with the saber bearers.

If an arch is held inside, ushers line up with the bridal party at the altar. After the final blessing, the bride and groom turn to face the guests and remain there while the saber bearers get into position. The senior saber bearer will issue a very quiet cue to the other Soldiers and they will all turn, proceed to the center aisle in pairs, and face the guests. They will stop just forward from the first pew or row. With the command "Center Face," they pivot so that the Officers are in two lines facing each other. At the Arch Saber's command, the saber is raised until it touches the tip of the saber directly opposite. Guests will stand and the bride and groom will pass beneath the arch and start the processional. With the commands "Carry Sabers, Rear Face, Forward March," the saber bearers will move outdoors to prepare for the second arch. The guests will follow behind the bridal couple toward the exit door. After the arch is formed, the bride and groom will pass under the saber arch. The last two Officers to make up the arch will lower their swords in front of the couple to detain them. The recessional continues after the saber bearers have exited the chapel.

Uniformity

One last thing, if you plan on walking under the arch of sabers, either the bride or groom should be in uniform. If the bride is a military member marrying a civilian and opts to wear a traditional wedding gown or civilian clothing, she should seriously consider if it is appropriate to include a saber arch in the ceremony. Although this has been allowed, many believe it is odd and inappropriate to have two civilians walk under the arch of sabers.

At the Reception

If the groom is in uniform, protocol dictates that he precede the bride in the receiving line. If you would like, national colors and distinguishing flags may be displayed, exactly centered, behind the receiving line (check with any battalion headquarters and they will direct you to a Protocol Officer who will locate these for you). After guests have greeted the bride, groom, and members of the receiving line, it is time to cut the cake. Rather than have the arch of sabers inside the church or chapel during the recessional, some couples opt to have the arch included at the reception hall. If this is the case, after the receiving line, on command, the saber bearers enter the reception room and line up in front of the wedding cake, facing each other. The bride and groom leave the receiving line and pass beneath the arch. They may pause and kiss before proceeding to cut the cake. The groom will hand the bride his unsheathed saber, place his hand over hers and help her cut the cake. Don't bother with the baby's breath or tulle; there is no ornamentation allowed on the saber. If you prefer to save the cake-cutting until after dinner, simply leave out the arch of sabers and cut the cake with the saber as directed above. And please note: there can be no cake in the face when either the bride or groom is in uniform. This is a recent tradition which has no place in a military wedding, or any other weddings as far as I'm concerned.

A Different Kind of "Taps"

Although it isn't official tradition, civilian brides should be aware that the sword bearer on the right may give you a gentle swat on the behind with his sword and say, "Welcome to the Army Mrs. _____." If this happens to you (as it happened to me), please don't let your "I am woman" sensibilities overtake you. It is part of the deal. If you make a fuss about it, you will come off as a person who does not respect military tradition. Besides, in fifty years, you will wish for a handsome young Soldier to give you a swat on the rear end.

A Typical Informal Event

The most common types of informal events are change-of-command ceremonies, company-sponsored events held at the armory such as family day, holiday parties, award, retirement, and promotion ceremonies, or parades and programs held in conjunction with conferences and conventions.

Informal events in the military are just like informal events in the civilian world. Although the themes and occasions vary, the relaxed and casual atmosphere is constant. The only thing you need to do is mind your manners, mingle with different people, and have a good time (within reason). Don't wear your Soldier's rank. Treat everybody with respect.

I am not going to waste time trying to explain how informal events are structured. There is so much variety and very few rules. If you would like more information about the basic structure of a change-of-command ceremony, it can be found in the "What if my Spouse is the Company Commander?" chapter.

Okay . . . I'm Sold.
How Do I Get Myself on the Invite List?

Hopefully, you will be invited to events sponsored by your Soldier's company or battalion. If this isn't the case and if you enjoy attending parties and events, a wonderful way to do this is to make sure your Soldier is an active member in professional organizations. The two most popular organizations are The National Guard Association of the United States (NGAUS) and the Enlisted Association of the National Guard of the United States (EANGUS). Both are nonpartisan organizations. Every state has its own state association as part of NGAUS and EANGUS. Both Commissioned Officers and NCOs are expected to pay reasonable dues to both their state association as well as the national organization. The dues structure is prorated by rank. The dues are used to pay for lobbying trips to

---

Other Tips for Incorporating Military Traditions into Your Weddings

- Incorporate a patriotic hymn into your ceremony. If you look in your church hymnal, you will find a lot of options. "The Battle Hymn of the Republic" makes an excellent recessional.
- Make sure that you alert your photographer in advance to any military moments that you want captured on film. If you are including the arch of sabers, tell the photographer exactly when and where it will happen.
- If you have a local Guard band, hire the members to play dance music at your reception. Even though they are playing as a private band, they will come in uniform and your guests will enjoy this extra special touch.

Washington, D.C. to further military construction funds, communication tools for membership (website), administrative support, and supplies. Every state budget is very small and every penny spent is carefully scrutinized by a volunteer Board of Directors. Unless your Soldier is involved on the state Board of Directors or as a volunteer for a particular program or event, there isn't a time commitment expected with annual membership. Your state Guard leadership will be involved in this organization and the networking is very valuable for Soldiers to get to know their senior leaders and to learn the politics behind the scenes. From a spouse's perspective, this is a chance to meet people from all across the state and beyond. It is also a great opportunity to meet members of the Air Guard and their spouses.

From a strictly social perspective, both of these professional organizations host annual state and national conferences that typically include a formal banquet/ball as well as informal spouse's brunches, golf tournaments, and casual mixers. There will definitely be a hospitality room set up and you will get a lot of bang for your buck. Conferences include business sessions (typically occurring over a Friday and Saturday afternoon) where members review and vote on legislative issues and their priority for presentation to either state or national legislative bodies. This means that your Soldier will have to mix business with pleasure a bit. Never fear, there will be plenty of fun events planned for you to attend on your own. The people who plan these conferences work very hard to make them enjoyable and entertaining. Many conferences are held on resorts or other desirable locations. If professional development is offered at the state conference, Soldiers can come on orders and get paid for travel costs and one day of pay. However, lodging and fees for events are not covered. Depending on the level of the conference, you should plan on budgeting $250-$500 to attend. In my opinion, this is money well spent and we put this in our annual budget. Be warned, these events fill up very quickly. If you want to attend, you must be prompt with your response and your payment. Details about events and activities are sent via e-mail or regular mail. If you wait too long, the hotel may fill up or you will not get the negotiated rate. There is usually an overflow hotel designated, but I prefer to be in the center of the action.

Unofficial Events

While some Guard families are lucky enough to have other Guard families in their community, for many others, you are on your own. After living in my community for seven years, besides my friend Lynn, I have yet to meet another Guard family out and about. When my husband was in command, I would have loved to have hosted different types of social events in our home. But we lived more than an hour from the armory and knew that asking people to work their way through Atlanta traffic for a tea would be a burden. In addition, Guard members work full-time civilian jobs and so do many of their spouses. Extra events can impose on people's already limited free time. But this does not mean that you can't make an effort to socialize with people. Even though people are busy, don't let that stop you from planning a special event on your own. I enjoy official events but there isn't anything that means more than being invited into somebody's home. When I worked in the architectural industry, we had a lot of corporate events. There were events at art galleries, annual holiday parties, off-site conferences, etc.

NGAUS and EANGUS

Formed in 1878, The National Guard Association of the United States (NGAUS) represents nearly 45,000 current and former Army and Air National Guard Officers. The organization is focused on procuring better equipment, standardized training, and a more combat-ready force by petitioning Congress for resources. See www.ngaus.org for more information.

The Enlisted Association of the National Guard of the United States (EANGUS) was formally organized in 1972 with the goal of increasing the voice of enlisted persons in the National Guard. EANGUS has a constituency base of over 414,000 Soldiers and Airmen, their families, as well as thousands of retired members. See www.eangus.org for more information.

But my favorite event was the holiday party that the CEO hosted at his house. It was always casual, relaxed, and fun. Home is where the heart is and it's nice to see people in their natural habitats. During my husband's command, although the company had a holiday party for all the Soldiers at the armory, I wanted to do something special for the Officers and their significant others. After talking over possible options, we decided to throw a formal Captain's Call dinner party at our home. I brought out the good china, moved the furniture around, and stashed the kids upstairs with some DVDs. The party was a ton of work but it is one of the best things I have done as an Army spouse. I treated the attendees to a seven-course meal that I planned and prepared myself. It was worth all the time and I would definitely do it again. Whether it is a casual backyard barbeque, a New

Helpful Hints and Practical Ideas for Entertaining

- Welcome home party for Soldier deployed abroad or a surprise appreciation cocktail party for a Soldier deployed on homeland duty
- Veterans Day Dinner
- Traditional New Year's Day open house hosted by Colonels and above
- Promotion party for Soldiers promoted at the same time
- Seated dinners, buffets, picnics
- Heavy appetizers or desserts
- Ice cream social, cookouts
- Brunch, luncheons, potlucks
- Craft nights or a Bring an Unfinished Craft to Work on Party
- BYOT Party (Bring Your Own Topping to share—for baked potatoes, pizza, ice cream sundaes)
- Come as You Were When Invited Party
- Show and Tell Party (Guests bring wedding albums, high-school yearbooks, or baby pictures.)
- Wives' Dining In
- Wine tasting

(Adapted from: It Takes a Team: A Resource for the Company Commander's Spouse/Representative U. S. Army War College, 1996.)

Accessed August 20, 2010, http://www.carlisle.army.mil/usawc/dclm/take/index.htm

Year's Day open house, or an ice cream party at the armory, your efforts will be appreciated, especially by your Soldier.

If you are lucky enough to be invited to a private party, try your best to attend. Organizing a social event is a lot of work and it can be costly. So, people want a good turnout. Just remember one thing, unless your children's names are printed on the envelope or they are specifically invited by the host or hostess, they are not invited. Don't put your hostess on the spot by asking if they are invited or bringing them along. If you are unable to get a sitter; decline the invitation. There is no need to mention your childcare issues to the hostess. It will only make her feel bad!

Who to Invite

If you decide to host an event, who you invite depends on the occasion. In the Guard, it is perfectly acceptable to mix together civilian friends and Guard friends. Certainly, if a Soldier is coming home from deployment, both should be invited. If you are hosting a promotion party for your Soldier, ask your Soldier to make up a list of who he or she would like to invite. They will know the politics involved and the appropriate people to extend an invitation to. It is fine to invite their superiors; they can choose whether or not to attend. If people can't attend, don't take it personally. Everybody is busy and Guard folks are particularly busy.

Wrap Up:

- Attending Guard events and incorporating military traditions into your own life are a good way to meet new people and feel extra-connected to your Soldier.
- The rules of etiquette are clearly documented and widely available. Check out the books available at your local library or bookstore and other resources available online.
- There are only two types of events: formal and informal. What you choose to wear depends on what your Soldier is told to wear.
- Casual events are relaxed and you need only go with the flow. Formal events such as a banquet or a Dining Out follow a predictable format. Familiarize yourself with the order of the program in advance.
- If you are invited to a Dining Out, go! It is an unforgettable experience and you are one of the lucky people who get to witness this unique military tradition first-hand.
- If you are planning a wedding to a member of the National Guard, don't miss the opportunity to incorporate military traditions into your wedding day. Your guests will enjoy this as much as you do.
- Do some proactive entertaining on your own. There are many great military traditions that can be creatively adapted for Guard life.

Chapter 10

When Your Soldier Deploys: Your Plan For Deployment

If it has not already happened, it will, whether you want it to or not. Even if your Soldier has been overseas already, that doesn't mean he or she is done. At some point, they will be called to duty again. Deep down inside, we accept this reality and from time-to-time, we entertain thoughts about making them get out. But we know that this won't solve anything. Our Soldiers want to serve and need our support. We both serve a cause that is bigger than ourselves.

Deployment is your opportunity to show your fellow citizens what it means to be in the Guard family. And, if you can get through a long-term deployment, you can get through just about anything. How do you do it?

Anybody who has ran a marathon will tell you that you must follow a mileage buildup schedule and be in tip-top physical condition. In Guard terms this means that you must tap into all the family program resources available and go through deployment processing so your paperwork is in order.

But even with that done, there will still be obstacles during the actual race. How do you push through a hamstring cramp at mile seventeen, an aching toe at mile nine, or the blisters that get more and more tender as you approach the finish line? Unfortunately, the Guard can't help you with that. You will have to do that for yourself.

I know what you are thinking: "Me? Like I don't have enough to do!" It is so true. The good news is that if you follow the plan presented in this chapter, you will find that there are people ready, willing and happy to help you during deployment. But more on that later.

Deployment Processing

We learned about Family Programs Offices (FPO), Family Assistance Centers (FAC), and Family Readiness Groups (FRG) in the previous chapter. They are the big three and can answer any questions you have about deployment. They know where the best resources are, both online and in-person. Your unit's FRG will coordinate pre-deployment information sessions and workshops. As the deployment draws near, there will be an official program, typically held in the evening at the armory, where family members gather to meet with leaders from the state's FPO and other representatives. You will learn about everything from how pay works to how benefits are administered. Plan in advance and, if possible, get a babysitter. These sessions can last several hours and you will be given a ton of information. If you feel completely overwhelmed, don't worry. You can review the handouts on your own time and your FAC will be there to answer any follow-up questions that you have.

During deployment processing, you will also learn about wonderful resources available to help you understand everything from the emotional phases of deployment to recognizing the symptoms of Post Traumatic Stress Disorder. You will also be introduced to an important new resource, the Rear Detachment Command.

The Rear Detachment Command

The Rear Detachment Command is a stay-behind link between Soldiers, their families, and all the Army and ARNG resources and equipment necessary to support their mission. Typically, the Rear Detachment Command which is led by the Rear Detachment Commander, or RDC, will set up shop in the deployed unit's armory. Soldiers serving in this capacity take over the responsibilities of deployed staff. The Rear Detachment Commander:

- Serves as unit commander during deployment
- Maintains regular contact with deployed unit

- Helps resolve family readiness problems or refers them to appropriate post agencies
- Is the link between the FRG and military resources

In addition to administrative responsibilities and overseeing logistics and supply operations, the RDC is the official information source for families. They conduct information sessions for family members, maintain regular contact with FRG leadership, validate and maintain Family Care Plans, and assist with FAC operations when necessary. The RDC is a conduit for timely and accurate information and assistance to families and FRG groups. If you hear information and don't know if it is true, verify it with the RDC. One of a spouse's biggest concerns during a deployment is how to contact the Soldier in case of an emergency situation. The RDC is in the know and maintains contact with the leadership of the deployed unit and, in urgent situations, can pass messages to the unit for relay to your Soldier. An urgent situation would include the birth of a child or other important family matter that can't wait. In case of an absolute emergency, the American Red Cross manages the contact process. To assess whether a situation is an emergency or not, consider this: emergency messages should only be sent for situations that would require an emergency leave situation during training or deployments. Emergencies include a serious illness, impending death, or death of an immediate family member. To get in touch with your Soldier, you will need to know your Soldier's Social Security Number, rank, unit, military address, names of the commander or First Sergeant, unit phone numbers, and temporary duty (TDY) or deployment location. The Red Cross will work through military channels to get in touch with your Soldier; however, it is up to the military whether or not your Soldier may return home. If it is determined that your Soldier needs to come home, and this is confirmed by appropriate professionals (private doctor, military doctor), your Soldier will come home. As soon as the emergency passes, your spouse may return to his or her unit. All of this information will be explained, in detail, during deployment processing.

From Weekend Warrior to Title 10 Status

The most important family action item during pre-deployment is to complete the necessary paperwork to get both the Soldier and their dependents into the system. As you know, when your Soldier changes to a

Title 10 status, he or she becomes equal to a full-time, active duty service member in the eyes of the military. In turn, the spouse and dependants of Title 10 Guardsmen are granted the same benefits as an Active Army family. Your Soldier will receive a paycheck twice a month (or once a month if you select that option) that, in addition to fulltime Basic Pay, will include Basic Allowance for housing. This is tax-free and depending on your Soldier's rank and where you live, can range from hundreds to thousands of dollars per month. Another huge change is that a Soldier's spouse and dependants are eligible for comprehensive medical and dental benefits. During pre-deployment, your unit or battalion will plan a comprehensive session to get you and your family into the system. You will be given an official military photo identification, register in DEERS, sign up for SGLI or a similar group life insurance, and update all beneficiary information.

The Family Care Plan

Every Soldier has to prepare for mobilization and make sure their family is taken care of in their absence. If they have not done so already, your Soldier should create a Family Care Plan (FCP) (DA Form 5305-R). Some units require that every member have an updated FCP on file. Some Soldiers, such as those who are single parents or dual military couples, are required to complete a FCP. Even if you are not required to complete a FCP and even if deployment isn't on the horizon, I would highly encourage every Guard family to develop a formal FCP. The most important part of an FCP is to assign a guardian for your family in case of emergency. The guardian needs Power of Attorney to act on behalf of your Soldier and yourself and has access to necessary funds. Sit down with your guardian and discuss their responsibilities and arrange for necessary travel and escort to transfer family members to their guardian. Most of the forms may be found online or through your Soldier's unit. Work on this together. Have your Soldier file a copy with his or her unit, retain a copy for your personal records and give a copy to a friend or family member. You may never need it but it will provide a framework to talk about some of the issues that arise during deployments. It is a chance to make sure that you are on the same page. Most importantly, it is a proactive way to make sure that you have a plan in place in case of a short-term or long-term deployment.

The Long Haul: A Unique Plan Just for Guard Spouses

There are entire books written about deployment that go through what to expect during each and every phase. There are government publications that tell us exactly what your unit's RDC does and how he or she can help the families of deployed Soldiers. There are FRGs providing support and assistance to unit family members. There are hundreds of excellent articles and checklists on www.militaryonesource.com that discuss every aspect of deployment. You have attended all the meetings. Read all the books. The key websites are book marked on your favorites list. The important phone numbers are stuck on the refrigerator door. You have your deployment checklist. But what now? Why do you still feel so scared? Or, if you Soldier is already overseas, why do you feel so lost and lonely? Well, because in my opinion, the Army misses the mark when it comes to understanding what Guard spouses really need when it comes to a long-term deployment. There. I have said it. The system simply wasn't designed specifically for our unique hybrid civilian/ military needs.

We live and work on Main Street, USA. Many of us are the only military family within our communities. Of course, we have our fellow Guard spouses to commiserate with (although many of our fellow Guard spouses don't live anywhere near us), but how can the members of our FRG help us when they are going through the SAME THING that we are?

A Great Guard Read

Who would think that a woman addicted to *Better Homes and Gardens* and *US Weekly* would take such a shine to a military magazine. Well, the thing is, GX: *The Guard Experience* magazine does not come off as military. The editors understand that Guardsmen are both civilians and Soldiers and this is reflected in the tone and content of the magazine. It is well-designed, easy to read, and yes, it is hip! The articles are always interesting and well-reported. And, they always include items of interest to family members. If your Soldier gets this magazine, don't be so fast to hand it off. After my husband reads it from cover to cover, he leaves old copies of GX at the barber shop, oil change place, and doctor's office. He thinks this is a great way to show off the Guard. I agree. www.national guardcom/life/gx-the-guard-experience

They can't give you a break from your children when you are at your wits end, pick up a gallon of milk when you have run out, shovel your sidewalk, or make up for the missed holidays, special occasions, or just the daily comfort of having your Soldier home with you. And, if your Soldier is deployed to a war-zone, they can't take away the what-ifs that occupy your thoughts from the moment that you kiss them goodbye.

Every Guard family member needs a concrete support system at the ready to help them during deployment. This chapter provides an action plan that was developed especially with YOU in mind. Because when it really comes down to it, it is up to you and your Soldier to create and implement a plan for deployment. You have to figure out a way to anticipate your needs before you become overwhelmed or depressed. I hope that you find some new information that you have not seen before and will take away a few tips that will help ease the burden during your Soldier's deployment.

They Mean Well, But . . .

As hard as people try, they simply can't understand how tough deployment is for the families of Citizen-Soldiers.

People who think that having your Soldier deployed is comparable to being involved in a long-distance relationship or having a spouse that travels frequently, just don't get it. There are four key differences:

- Our spouses leave for long stretches of time. If they are overseas, we can miss an entire calendar year of holidays and special occasions
- Communication with our loved one is unpredictable, brief, and sporadic
- Many of our Soldiers are working within a war zone
- Our Soldier's business travel does not include free breakfast at the Holiday Inn and phone calls between meetings

It is very hard for people to understand. But that does not mean they don't want to help. One of the most challenging parts of deployment is turning people's good intentions into actions and sustaining momentum.

Does This Sound Familiar?

The first two weeks of a deployment, you have more help and support than you know what to do with. Your phone rings off the hook, your freezer is filled with lasagna and people are eager to do anything and everything they can do to help ease your burden. Your friends and family members are motivated and on the job. You, on the other hand, are operating within a strange cloud of denial. You are going through the motions with mixed feelings. You are too off your game to try and pin helpers down for long-term support. After about a month, reality sets in. You realize that your Soldier is going to be gone for a long time. At the same time, you sadly notice that your friends and family members (if you are lucky enough to live near family) have moved on. Their lives are not affected the way that yours is and as time passes, they assume that you are moving on too. They don't understand that even though you are putting on a brave face, that you are living a life that isn't yours. You may be lonely or overwhelmed. If you have kids, you are probably exhausted from trying to make things seem normal and keep some semblance of routine. You know that you have to define a new normal and go on with your life. You have to take care of yourself and stay strong for the sake of your family. That is a lot to think about and you need help! Now! You're ready to take all of the help that was so kindly offered when the word came down that your Soldier was leaving. You wait for the phone to ring and e-mails to pour in. But, hold on, wait a second . . .

Uh . . . where the heck is everybody? Well, they are doing their own thing. And that's okay because everybody is busy and everybody has their own challenges to deal with. But just because they move on, does not mean you need to be left behind. I truly believe that most people want to do something to help Soldiers and their families. When people say things like, "If there is anything I can do to help, let me know," and then seem to disappear off the face of the earth, don't write them off. Give them the benefit of the doubt and offer opportunities for them to help you. But it isn't that simple, is it?

As much as we would all like an endless army of do-gooders at our beck and call, life just does not work like that. The fact is that if you don't ask for help, you should not expect it. Just remember, even if our friends and families want to help us, the whole experience is new to them and they don't know what to do. And, they don't want to take on more than they can handle. As super agent, Jerry McGuire said to a legend in his own mind, Rod Tidwell, "Help me, help you." When it comes to deployment, those four words are the secret to unlocking the support you need.

The Biggest Obstacle

So, let's start by tackling the first problem. That would be YOU. Yes, YOU. It's true. When it comes to asking for and getting help during deployments, you are your own worst enemy. Guard families are a tough, proud bunch. Many of us don't like to ask for help. In fact, many people (you know who you are) hate asking for help and refuse to do so. My husband gets on my case about this all the time. "Why don't you just ask so and so?" Well, because I just don't want to . . . so whatever.

There is a part of me that feels like I need to save my favors for when I really need them. A deployment is an ideal time to cash in banked favors. The first thing you need to do is change your perspective. Most of the military spouses that I know believe that if people really do want to help, they will do so without prompting. That isn't realistic. Basically, when it comes to helping people out, there are five types of people in the world:

1. Those who say they will help but really don't want to help ("I wish I could help, but . . . ")
2. Those who offer help but put the ball back in your court ("If there is anything you need . . . call me.")
3. Those who offer help on their own terms ("If there is anything you need I will do it . . . as long as it does not disrupt by schedule.")
4. Those who help you, but make you feel guilty about it (You: "So how were the kids?" Them: "Well, actually they were pretty naughty.")
5. Those who are always there, ready and willing to help with anything.

As far as the last group of people, they are a rare and precious bunch. And because they are so giving, they are probably overextended. Hey, I'm not one of those people and you probably are not either. If I'm being completely honest, I would fall into category three. I am open to helping people but there are some favors that I just can't do with my schedule. In addition to my creative projects, I work a corporate job from home. And even though people assume that if you are at home, in any capacity, you are available, that simply isn't the case. Because it is difficult for me to field personal phone calls during the day (the calls that try and beep through when I am on a conference call), I'm not the best person to call when you need a shoulder to cry on. Chances are I've got one eye on my e-mail and another on the clock. But, that doesn't mean I'm not willing to help on my own terms.

While I can't help with childcare (or much else during the weekday), I am happy to make a gourmet meal and drop it off once a month (and I have a bunch of friends that I can hit up to do the same). I am happy to pick up a few things at the grocery store while shopping. I am happy to take a child or two overnight every few months. Think about your own schedule and preferences. Wouldn't it be nice if people let you help in a way that you didn't resent?

My point is, don't rule out the other types. They can help you too. The key is to tap your network (and the network of your friends and family members) and take whatever help you can get on their terms. Different types of assistance add up over the course of a deployment.

Your PALs: A Personal Assistance League

How do you find and organize a crew to help you for the entire duration of a deployment? What if you live far from a family and only have a few close friends? Who are these do-gooders who will bring you meals and help you with things you don't have time to do? How do you get the help you need without putting people on the spot?

Meet your PALs. A PAL is a Personal Assistance League made up of friends, family, and community members who are ready, willing, and eager to help you throughout the duration of a deployment. The PAL concept was inspired by an amazing initiative that Mary Pawlenty, the former First Lady of Minnesota, implemented to help Minnesota's military families. The First Lady's Military Family Care Initiative (www.militaryfamilies.state. mn.us/index.php) connects service, community, and faith-based organizations with the families of deployed Soldiers. Each volunteer group specifies the services that they are willing to provide and Guard family members go to a centralized website and can search for the type of help that they need and find organizations in their area that provide assistance in that area. The Guard member contacts the group and coordinates the process. When I saw this program, I was floored. I thought "Boy, she really gets it." If every Guard family had, say, 25 people signed on and willing to do only two things over the course of a year, what a difference it would make. If we can deploy our own support resources in this way, there would be a person to cheer us on at every mile marker.

This support system is called a Personal Assistance League. Your PAL will:

- Pick up where military resources leave off
- Provide consistent support and encouragement
- Be custom built according to your specific needs
- Be in the trenches with you for the duration of your Soldier's deployment
- Begin with your friends and extended family members
- Grow through word of mouth (she told two friends, and they told to friends, and so on . . .)
- Achieve consistent momentum through community outreach

Your support system will be made up of friends, family members, and, most importantly, strangers. But it will begin with you.

Setting Up Your PAL

Your goal is to build a robust and official support system with members who are doing small things occasionally. For example, your sister may have her hands full in the late afternoons and evenings helping her kids with homework or coordinating their activities. But if she is free during the days, maybe her assignment can be to watch your kids when you have an appointment. Your single girlfriend may travel a lot for business and not have the time to see you often. But if she loves to bake, she may be a good person to make Valentine cut-out cookies with your kids when you don't have the energy to keep that family tradition alive. Your co-worker may not want to hang out with you and your kids on the weekend, but he may be the perfect person to plan a special gathering to celebrate your birthday and make sure you have a ride to and from so you can have a glass of champagne (or two) and enjoy yourself. People from the church may be willing to bring over a meal once a month. Your local American Legion may be able to help you rake leaves. Your Mom may want to help you trim your tree and decorate your house for Christmas when you are sad and don't feel very festive. A local Guard family (whose Soldier is home) can escort you to a banquet or Dining Out so you can dress up and socialize with members of the Guard family. The examples go on and on. When you add all of this piecemeal assistance together with the consistent, steadfast assistance provided by a few very special people, you have got yourself a pretty decent support system. Sound good? Of course! Good enough to start asking for help? That's what I thought. Well, don't worry. The good news is that you will not be asked to go door to door with a sign around your neck that says "Help me." Your PAL will do that for you.

But Not So Fast–You're Not Off the Hook Yet

You know that your PAL starts with you. But there is another resource that you need to activate before you can relax: your Soldier. Your Soldier has a moral and legal responsibility to take care of his or her family during deployment. I don't care how busy they are, they need to help you set up your PAL. If your Soldier is already deployed, he or she can still help you build your PAL via e-mail. The first thing the two of you will do is find three key people to form your inner support circle:

- The Mother Hen–this is a proactive and persistent person who will do the asking on your behalf.
- The Dragon Slayer–this is an on-call person who will tackle unforeseen emergencies in your home.
- Nanny 911–this is a person who you can call last-minute who will take your children in case of emergency.

While other members of your PAL will provide different support functions sporadically, your inner circle will agree, in advance, to assist you with the three very specific and important functions.

Pal 1: The Mother Hen

The leader of your PAL is what Kathie Hightower and Holly Scherer, authors of "Help! I'm a Military Spouse, I Get a Life Too!" (www.militaryspousehelp.com) call the "Mother Hen." The Mother Hen single-handedly destroys a deployed spouse's biggest obstacle: unwillingness to ask for help. The Mother Hen's main role is to do the asking on your behalf. We all have a friend or a family member who seems to know everybody in town. They are the type of person who knows how to get people to do things. They are bold individuals who are not afraid to ask people for things. In their mind, the worst thing that can happen is that they will be told "No." But that does not discourage them. They will keep at it until they hear the answer they want, which is, of course, "Yes."

We all know somebody like this. They have probably hit us up for a thing or two over the years. This is the perfect person to be your Mother Hen. Hopefully, this person will surface without much prompting. It's very likely that when word starts to spread that your Soldier has an impending deployment, there will be a few people who make it clear that they really, really want to help you. You know that they aren't just saying that they want to help, but that they actually do want to help. These are excellent people to approach about being your Mother Hen. Due to proximity, a neighbor will make an ideal Mother Hen. If you are worried about soliciting a Mother Hen, don't be. It is an important job but most people want to help a military family. A smart Mother Hen knows that they will not have a problem finding volunteers. They are up for the challenge. The Mother Hen will begin to form your PAL before your Soldier deploys. They will begin to tap into both your network and their own. They will work with you and your Soldier to develop a calendar that tracks appointments, travel, family occasions, and other activities. Throughout the deployment, they will check in with you once a week to see how you are doing and find out what type of help you need. They will keep your PAL informed via e-mail or telephone. It is important that your Mother Hen stay focused on finding and motivating a group of volunteers to help you and your family. They need to keep people motivated so you have a constant support system in place throughout the duration of the deployment. The longer your Soldier is gone, the harder the job is. This is all a nice way of saying don't activate your Mother Hen for anything besides Mother Hen duty.

If you don't have an obvious candidate to be your Mother Hen, you will need to get creative. Here are some suggestions:

- Call your church and other local churches. Talk to the priest or pastor and see if they have any suggestions.
- Contact your local American Legion or VFW post. Retired military family members make excellent Mother Hens.
- If you live in a neighborhood with a Homeowner's Association, get in touch with someone on the Board of Directors and have them spread the word.
- Check with your local Chamber of Commerce. Many business organizations in military communities (especially where units are located) have Military Affairs representatives.

- Contact the FRG leader at the nearest non-deployed unit. She may be able to offer you some suggestions. You may also be able to find a Guard family in your community whose Soldier isn't deployed. They may be willing to take on this role (and you can return the favor when their time comes).

By the way, every Guard spouse who I have talked to about this concept says the same thing, "I would have loved having a Mother Hen. And I would do it in a heartbeat for somebody else."

Cold Calling Your Mother Hen

Here are some tools that will help you secure a Mother Hen if you are approaching an organization:

Via phone:

"My husband is going on deployment for x months. I am working on setting up what I call a PAL–a Personal Assistance League. This is a group of people who can provide some light assistance during the deployment. Like most Guard spouses, I am not very comfortable asking for help so bear with me if I sound nervous. To get my PAL started, I need to find a Mother Hen. This is a person who knows people in the community and is willing to reach out to them on my family's behalf. Most of this can be done via e-mail and it should not require more than a couple hours of work per week. The Mother Hen's main job is to do the asking. Would you happen to have any ideas that would help me find a Mother Hen?"

Via e-mail:

> Hello, I am the wife of a Guardsman. We are trying to set up a PAL support system for our family. This is a Personal Assistance League (PAL) made up of community members who are willing to provide some occasional assistance to our family. Like most Guard spouses, I am not comfortable asking for help. Of course, my friends and family members will be a part of my PAL, but my goal is not to overwhelm them. I would like to call on them when I need more urgent support. But I

know that there are people in the community who may be interested in helping a military family. To get my PAL started, I need to find a Mother Hen. This is a person who knows people in the community and is willing to reach out to them on my family's behalf. Most of this can be done via e-mail and it shouldn't require more than a couple hours of work per week. They won't be providing the assistance themselves, but rather, will help grow the PAL through their own network. If you know anybody in your organization who may be willing to take on this responsibility, please feel free to pass my contact information on to them. I really appreciate your time.

Sincerely,
First Name, Last Initial
City
Phone Number

Pal 2: The Dragon Slayer

The second person you need to line up is your "Dragon Slayer." The Dragon Slayer takes care of unforeseen obstacles. Let me give you an example. When my husband was away on Army business, my dog, Rumsfeld, started acting really weird in the middle of the night. I could hear him sniffing and whining downstairs. I was petrified. After lying in my bed, paralyzed in fear (okay, perhaps I am being a little dramatic) I finally got up my courage to investigate. He was sniffing at the fireplace and the wall. He was growling and would not come when I called him. I figured that some type of animal was trapped in the chimney. I prayed that this animal would stay trapped in the chimney, at least until morning. I was in a panic. I can deal with overflowing toilets and other household mishaps, but if there is any type of creature in or near my house that I haven't personally procured, I fear for my life. Eventually, Rummy came upstairs and I wasn't attacked by a rogue squirrel. We survived the night. But the next morning I knew that Jon and I needed a person on call when he is away. We needed a Dragon Slayer.

Water coming in the basement in the middle of the night? Garage door jammed? Storm blow a tree through your window? Rogue rodent? Don't know who to call? Now you do.

If you are lucky enough to live near family, this is an easy person to identify. Your father, brother, brother-in-law are all good candidates. If you are far from family, finding a Dragon Slayer can be a bit of a challenge because it simply isn't safe or smart to have any men in your house when you are alone who you don't know personally. If you don't have a Dragon Slayer in your Rolodex, approach safe organizations and find a person who you feel comfortable with. I have two Dragon Slayers: my long-time handyman, Terry, and a friend from our local American Legion, a retired Army Colonel.

Pal 3: Nanny 911

If you have children, you will need a Nanny 911. This angel provides childcare in case of an emergency or unforeseen circumstance. This isn't a person to watch your children while you are getting your nails done or going on a business trip. This is the person who will come over to your house and sit with your children if you (or one of your children) need to go to the emergency room in the middle of the night. A Nanny 911 will pick your kids up from the bus stop if you get in a fender bender on your way home from work and can't make it on time. If you wake up with a terrible flu and can barely dial the phone let alone watch your kids, this is the person who will come and pick them up–no questions asked. If one of your kids is sick and you absolutely can't miss work to stay home with them, your Nanny 911 will help you. Let us face it; this job is a huge responsibility that can be a bit of a drag. This is a hard type of help to ask for. But if you and your Soldier do this in advance, the person will not be put on the spot.

You will need to find somebody who isn't only willing to take on this responsibility but has a flexible enough schedule to do so. Your mother, mother-in-law, sister, or sister-in-law are ideal candidates. If you don't have family nearby, you will need to find somebody through your church or other trustworthy networks. Of course, you need somebody who you can trust who is available. A retired neighbor may be willing to help you. But you must find somebody willing to help you before you end up in a very stressful situation. And, I would highly suggest that you only use Nanny 911 when you really need them (thus the 911). Hopefully, you will not need to use them at all.

Turning Good Intentions into Specific Actions

One of the most challenging parts of deployment is turning people's good intentions into actions and sustaining momentum. Typically, people are there during the initial weeks after our Soldiers depart, but very few people are with us for the long haul. They have their own lives to manage and it is hard to stay fired up during a year-long deployment. The more people you have in your PAL, the easier it will be to have a constant level of support. So, it is time to expand your PAL. Ideally, you will need 25 people, each willing to do two things over the course of a long deployment versus five people who are expected to be constantly on-call. The goal is to add little things together to give you help from the day your Soldier leaves to the day he or she comes home.

The first step is to provide your Mother Hen with three things:

- A list of at least ten people (the more, the better) who you know personally and may want to help. The closer they live to you, the better. Don't obsess about how frequently they can help you or what their specific preferences are, just come up with a list of names, phone numbers, and e-mails. The initial list should not only include your friends and family members but people who you have provided support to in the past. This isn't about payback. It is about letting people know your situation and giving them a chance to help you. They can always say no. And some people will. But since they are saying no to your Mother Hen, you will not take it as personally.

- A list, by month, of any known events, occasions, or appointments. Your list should include vacations, work travel, birthdays, anniversaries, social events, school events, out of town visitors, doctor's appointments, etc. When your Mother Hen looks at your calendar, she will see times when you may need extra support. If your child has a birthday coming up, you may need some extra help planning the party or a free hour or two to shop for gifts without prodding eyes. If your child is being confirmed, you may want some extra company at church to offset your Soldier's absence. On your birthday or wedding anniversary, you may want to have a small celebration with some of your PALs. Whatever the situation is, providing a list of key dates will help your PALs set aside the time you need. The more notice you can give your PALs, the better. Of course, your schedule will change frequently, but this will give your Mother Hen a place to start.

- A prioritized list of needs. You can't have everything, so focus on the top three types of support that will help you get through the deployment.

So, What, Exactly, Will I Need?

Figuring out the type of support that you need is a key part of a successful deployment strategy. Don't wait until you are in the thick of things to get the help you need. Your needs will depend on your situation. If you don't know what your needs are, start with a look at Mary Pawlenty's list:

- Babysitting
- Automobile assistance
- Handyman (minor home repairs)
- Help with chores
- Mow the lawn
- Organize a birthday party
- Paint or repair a fence
- Pet sit
- Plant flowers
- Rake the yard
- Prepare and deliver a gift basket
- Send care package to your Soldier
- Prepare and deliver meals
- Purchase and deliver groceries
- Send cards or letters of encouragement
- Shovel/plow sidewalks and driveways
- Stain decks
- Trim hedges
- Wash cars
- Wash windows
- Weed the yard

This list is effective because of its simplicity. It focuses on common needs and includes wish-list items such as care packages and stretch items such as staining the deck. I would suggest pinpointing three specific areas of assistance for every season that your Soldier is gone. Another way to pin down what you need is to spend a few weeks keeping a daily log of absolutely everything you do to manage your jobs, home, and family (do this before your Soldier deploys). This includes paying bills, running errands, car maintenance, homework patrol, carpooling, grocery shopping–everything. From that list, identify the things that YOU will continue doing. My list would include things like:

- Grocery shopping
- Planning and preparing meals
- Caring for children
- Running errands/getting kids to events and activities
- Housework/laundry
- Staying on top of household paperwork

Next, identify the items that your Soldier does. Here is my list:

- Paying bills
- Watching kids when I need a break or have extra work to do.
- Taking kids out for bike rides and other adventures
- Yard work
- Car maintenance

All items will move to one of three places:

- Onto your list
- Outsourced (budget willing)
- Your PAL

Combine your lists together and identify things that you can hire out while your Soldier is away. Next, make a list of things that you want to do that may fall by the wayside due to new responsibilities. Here is my list:

- Home improvement projects
- Housework/laundry
- Preparing healthy meals consistently
- Doing fun things with the kids

And, finally, make a list of things that will make you feel better when you are feeling down:

- Hair/nail/spa appointment
- Night out with friends who are willing to pick me up and drop me off so I can have a glass (or two) of wine
- Airport transportation so I can take the kids on an extended trip to visit out of town family
- Pet sitting in our home
- A friend or family member willing to accompany me to fun events–Guard and personal

Prioritizing is the key. Hey, I would love it if somebody would clean my house, do my laundry, watch my kids, weed my garden, and walk my dog whether my husband is deployed or not. But, the fact is that I can do most of these things myself. Some of the things that I can't do (mowing the grass, cleaning the gutters) will be hired out. That leaves a few things that I will really need help with (occasional childcare, meals and some people to socialize with once in awhile).

Remember, even though you are putting together a needs list, you may not get everything on your wish list. But anything is better than nothing. Your list will depend on your situation. If you are a homemaker with children, you will probably want an occasional break from the kids and help with yard work and other chores. If you are a working mother or father, you may want help dropping/picking kids up from school, running errands, and back-up childcare if you have to attend a special meeting or go on a business trip. If you are married without children, you may want help with home projects and some fun social activities to look forward to. If you are the parent of a Soldier, you may want your PAL to focus on giving you emotional support, sending care packages to your Soldier or accompanying you to FRG meetings and events.

The Ripple Effect

After reviewing your needs list, your Mother Hen will send an e-mail to the people who you have identified, as well as people in her own network that she feels may be interested in joining your PAL. A suggested format is shown here:

A LETTER FROM YOUR MOTHER HEN

Subject: Military PALs

Dear _____,

As some of you know, Jane Doe's husband will be deployed to (location) from (dates). Military spouses are very proud. Even though there is help available, they have a hard time asking for it. As a result, both the military spouse and their closest friends and family members start to feel overwhelmed. I have volunteered to be Jane's Mother Hen. My job is to build a support network to give her the support that she needs during the deployment. The only qualification you need to join Jane's Personal Assistance League, or PAL, is a desire to help the family. I know that there are good people in our community who love the military and want to offer their support. I also know that people are busy. Many people would like to help occasionally, when they have some spare time, but can't commit to anything more than that. Perhaps you don't think making a meal and dropping it off to the family once during a 12-month deployment is enough. Or that spending a few hours raking leaves makes a difference. But if we put all of these small things together, it makes a huge difference. We are grateful for any help that you can offer. My goal is to find 25 people who are willing to do two things during the duration of the deployment. If we add up this support, that means that Jane will have something to look forward to every week. If you want to do more than that, great! If you can't commit to that, I welcome any help that you can provide. My hope is that we can build an even larger support network. There are many ways to help this family and your suggestions are welcome. Here are some ways that the PAL could really make a difference to this family: *(Note: this section of the letter will be based on your specific needs; however, I have included a few examples that would apply to a family with children.)*

- Home-cooked, child-friendly meals are always appreciated. Perhaps you and a group of friends would enjoy gathering at one of the meal assembly businesses in the area.

- Jane works FT (or is home with her children FT) and, like all of us, she has her hands full. With her husband gone, she has more responsibilities. As a result, things can fall between the cracks. If you are going to the market, a quick phone call to check and see if there are any small items that you can pick up and drop off, would be a great help to her.
- The family has a five-year-old daughter and two-year-old son. If you know the family, play dates at your home, their home, or a local park are always appreciated. Even just an hour away from the kids gives Jane a chance to pay bills, run a quick errand, or write a letter to her husband.
- In the spring and fall, the family will need help raking leaves, trimming trees, and mulching garden beds. (Or in the winter, the family will need help shoveling the sidewalks.)

Even if you can't commit to helping, perhaps you know a friend, neighbor, co-worker, or fellow church member who would like to help this military family. Please let me know any people who you think would like to help. For security reasons, please don't forward this email. In addition, if you would be willing to post a flyer in your church or other organization, that would be a big help. Please e-mail me and I will forward the flyer to you. Jane knows how busy people are and does not want to inconvenience anybody or put them on the spot for help. In fact, if I were not asking on her behalf, I am certain she would not get any help for herself. But I know that people want to help and I want to give them an opportunity to do so. Whatever help you are able to provide is wonderful. Thank you for your time and consideration.

Sincerely,
Mother Hen

The flyer on the following pages is a great example of how to get community members to help Guard families. These aren't to be nailed onto telephone poles. They are meant to be displayed in churches or safe spots.

Your Mother Hen will track responses and collect contact information from volunteers. You now have the foundation to build a PAL. Remember, a PAL isn't a business and there isn't a special software program to track volunteers and schedule help. A PAL is a casual alliance of people who want

Want to Help the Family of a Deployed National Guard Soldier?

There is a National Guard family in our community that needs our help while their soldier is deployed.

We are looking for people to prepare child-friendly meals, help with yard work, and send care packages to the deployed soldier.

to help you while your Soldier is away. You and your Mother Hen will figure out the best way to manage your PAL as you go, through trial and error. They may even set up a "members only" Facebook page to keep all your PALS in touch. Be creative and leverage your own strengths to help your Mother Hen organize and manage your PAL. The more you can do to keep things rolling, the better.

The Worst Day

Perhaps the most important function a PAL plays is helping you through your "Worst Day." Your Worst Day is when you feel lonely and vulnerable.

Our MILITARY Kids, Inc. is a wonderful non-profit organization that provides substantial support in the form of grants to the children of National Guard and Military Reserve personnel who are currently deployed overseas, as well as the children of Wounded Warriors in all branches.

Grants can be used for all sorts of extracurricular activities (i.e. sports and fine arts) as well as tutoring. The eligibility requirements are:

- Parent must be deployed. Deployment must be for at least 180 days OCONUS (overseas), there are at least 60 days remaining on orders, AND child will start activity before service member returns home.
- Child is age 3 years through 12th grade.
- Grant will cover up to six months of future instruction, lessons, or tutoring for ONE activity/program with a maximum grant award of $500.00 per child. Grants are not available for activities that have already taken place.
- Only one check to one provider for the child's activity will be issued. Once a check has been issued to the provider, the activity may not be changed.
- Must declare that receipt of a grant will aid in easing a financial burden which would otherwise exist if expenses related to the child's activity were paid out of family funds.

To qualify for a grant, you must fill out an application and provide:

1) Title 10, mobilization/deployment orders (child is eligible as of "Report Date" on orders)
2) Child's military dependent ID card OR copy of birth certificate if the deployed service member is the biological parent of the child, OR Form 1172, Application for Uniformed Services Identification (DEERS Form). Contact your Family Assistance Representative or FRG leader for assistance in obtaining the DEERS form.
3) Program brochure, registration information, or letter from the service provider with mailing address, telephone number, and FEE for the activity.

If approved, Our Military Kids pays the activity provider directly and alerts the family. Hooah to this wonderful organization and their commitment to Guard children!
For more information contact:
www.ourmilitarykids.org

As Holly Golightly said in the movie *Breakfast at Tiffany's,* "The blues are because you're getting fat or because it's been raining too long. You're just sad, that's all. The mean reds are horrible. Suddenly you're afraid and you don't know what you're afraid of." That describes your worst day to a tee. During my husband's deployment, I made it through the weekdays without much trouble. At the time, I worked outside the home. My work kept me occupied and my co-workers were a great source of support for me. After work, I would pick the baby up from the sitter's house. I would feed her, play with her, bathe her, and put her in bed at 7:30 pm. I would work out on my elliptical machine and watch *Felicity* reruns on TV. After that, I would read a book or watch TV in bed until I fell asleep. Piece of cake. Saturdays were also manageable. I would run errands with the baby and spend time with friends if I felt like it. Again, I was fine. But come Sunday, the mean reds came on with a vengeance. Everybody was with their family and I didn't know what to do with myself. Looking back now, I should have gone to church with the baby and put a routine in place. But honestly, I avoided church because it made me feel even lonelier. One Sunday, a long holiday weekend when everyone I knew was out of town, I woke up and decided to kill some time via a trip to the outlet mall. I arrived at the mall at 9:30 only to find out that it didn't open until 11:00 am. I remember sitting in the car and sobbing. That was it! I completely broke down. After months of putting on a happy face, I lost it. I sat in the car and cried for a good ten minutes. I didn't know what to do with myself. Turn around and go home? Sit there and wait? It just seemed like it was one big Groundhog Day. Every day seemed so boring and lonely without Jon around. It seems kind of silly now. I mean, deployments are much longer now and the risk factor is much higher. But that is how I felt. It was a typical hopeless Sunday.

After about a month into the deployment, you too will probably notice a certain day of the week (or time of the day) when you get really, really down. We have all been there. Our energy level goes down, our self-pity goes up, and we start to worry and wonder "What if?" Don't worry, this is natural. Don't try and fight it. Hey, you are entitled. Your Soldier is gone! You are alone! And time is moving very, very slowly. Even though you don't need to pretend to be happy when you are not, you should still come up with a plan to take the edge off a bit. Shake things up a bit. Miss Golightly opted for a cab ride to Tiffany's. If that isn't possible, I would suggest designing a game plan for your worst day or time of the day.

For example, knowing now that Sundays were tough days for me, I made some changes. If my friend Lynn's husband was at drill, I would hang out with her and her daughter Hannah. I also planned in advance for special occasion and holiday weekends. A trip to Minnesota on my daughter's first birthday distracted me from the fact that Jon wasn't there to celebrate. I also get very overwhelmed from 5:00-7:30 pm or, what my grandmother calls the witching hours. Those crazy hours of homework, dinner, baths, story time, and clean up. And, for whatever reason, even though you are exhausted, your kids get a second wind and bounce around the house like fools. When Jon isn't on the scene, I change my witching hour routine. I get the kids bathed and fed by 5:00 pm. I rent a movie from the video store (one that they have not seen before . . . quite the challenge) and bring them into my room for movies and popcorn. I either sit with them or surf the internet or relax with a magazine. By the time the movie is over, they are ready for bed and I am ready to be alone. I make myself a cup of tea and watch TV in bed. You get the idea. Remember to let your Mother Hen know your worst day. They will have ideas to help you snap out of your funk and avoid the mean reds.

Safety First

Everybody has their own way of doing things, but personally, I don't think it is smart or safe to advertise when your Soldier is away. Women must be extra vigilant in this regard. Take a pass on the "Half My Heart Is in Afghanistan" bumper sticker. Save the yellow ribbons to welcome your Soldier home. Stay under the radar and get support through a trusted network. It is too bad that a few crazy people have to wreck everybody else's fun, but that is the world we live in. We have to maintain a careful balance between protecting the family with getting as much help as we can.

As far as your PAL is concerned, your Mother Hen is your liaison to the community at large. But how do you know who you can trust? My advice is to use common sense. If you know people, they can come to your house. If your friend knows a person and can vouch for them, they can come to your house. If a woman is dropping off a meal, she can come to your house. If you are not sure, pick up your casserole in a public place. If you are uncomfortable, have your Dragon Slayer on the scene when the guys from the Legion come to help with yard work. You don't need to be neurotic, but you do need to be careful. When in doubt–don't!

Thanking your PALs

Throughout the deployment, there are many ways to thank your PAL. With social networking this is very easy to do. It goes without saying that you need to send a timely, handwritten thank you note or make a call (or send an e-mail if you are really pressed for time) to anybody who goes out of their way to help you. Here are some other ways to thank your PAL:

- Ask your Soldier to e-mail your PALs consistently and give them an update on how he or she is doing. PALs love to receive photos of the troops.
- When your Soldier returns, include your PALs in your Soldier's welcome home party. Or, throw a PAL party just for them.
- Invite your PALs to any formal military functions that are open to civilians. What a great opportunity for them to attend an exclusive affair.

Testing your PAL

You don't have to wait for a year-long deployment to test your PAL. I tested my PAL when Jon was activated for Hurricane Katrina. Before he left, he called my core support system to let them know he was leaving and ask them if they could keep an eye on the family while he was away. That completely took the asking pressure off me. I received an invitation to bring the kids up for a Labor Day getaway weekend with friends. My PALs ordered me not to cook anything, buy anything, or bring anything. They went out of their way to help me that weekend so I could relax a little bit. The interesting thing is that just knowing that I had my core support resources standing by, ready to help me was a relief.

Sometimes I think half of the stress of being alone is the "What if this or that happens while he's away." Even if things go smoothly, you still worry about something going wrong. With your PAL in place, you will be more confident and ready to rise to the challenge. You have answered the question "What if?" and that provides instant peace of mind. If you really want to prepare yourself for deployment, take the journey with another Guard family. Be a Mother Hen. If you don't know a family personally, get in touch with your State Family Programs Office nearest FAC or FRG leader. Tell them what you want to do and ask them to put you in touch with a Guard family in need. Put systems in place to recruit volunteers and schedule assistance. Save every e-mail that you send and track lessons learned. Save all of this information for your Mother Hen. Not only will you have provided valuable assistance to a member of the Guard family, you will become an expert PAL and expand your own network.

The Rumor Mill

It is unfortunate that rumors run especially rampant during deployments. There is no question that deployments test relationships. I am a person who likes to see my husband as much as possible. He truly is my best friend. We like to talk, hang out, and be close. Even if we are not getting along on a particular day, I like to know that he is nearby so I can shoot him dirty looks. It also makes it easier to settle whatever the issue is and move on. When he is away, I get testy. I miss having him around and our day-to-day connection. It is enough of a challenge trying to balance romance with children. When you throw a long-term separation on top of that, you have to work five times as hard to stay connected. Although I am not in the military, I have worked in enough professional settings to know that some people view the workplace as a breeding ground for romance. After all, when you are working closely with people, share common goals, and spend a lot of time with them, you form relationships. That is just the way it is. But there is a difference between having a positive, professional relationship with members of the opposite sex and having a personal relationship with them. Many people don't understand boundaries and some have no respect for other people's marriages. The fact is that a deployment will intensify any feelings that you have. If either of you are insecure about your relationship or have issues concerning infidelity, the deployment will intensify these feelings. I would highly suggest attending some pre-deployment counseling sessions together. An impartial outsider will help you assess the situation and come up with a plan. If you are not willing to do this, you're setting yourself up for major issues down the road. Don't put yourself in this position. Even if you have a strong marriage, the sad truth is that there are some people in the world who have no respect for marriage. They like to flirt with a married man or woman just to see if they can get attention. If they think the person is feeling lonely or vulnerable, they will really turn up the heat. If you have ever had this happen in your marriage, you know how frustrating it is to have somebody following your spouse around like a lost puppy. Even though your spouse is innocent and didn't do anything to fuel the fire, it will still bug you. The best way to avoid this situation is to talk to your Soldier about it in advance. The strongest marriages have clear boundaries. Be loving, and by all means be direct:

- "I know that you have a great professional relationship with x and I think that's fine. But perception equals reality for a lot of people, especially if they are bored and want something to talk about. Don't set yourself up for rumor or speculation. I would really appreciate it if you socialize in groups versus one-on-one with any members of the opposite sex."
- "Just remember that even though I'm far away, I'm still your best friend. I know you feel the same way. I want you to know that you can come to me if you think somebody is trying to get too personal. I won't blame you but I want to know about it so we can figure out how to deal with it together."

Your Soldier may take offense. But, more likely, he or she will appreciate the fact that you are mature enough to bring the matter up. The same rules apply to you too. If you are one of those people who love to get negative attention by making your Soldier jealous, you need to stop it. Socialize with close friends and family members, and steer clear of people who don't support your marriage.

Dealing with the Media

As if deployment isn't tough enough, throughout the whole ordeal, we have the presence of 24-hour cable news and other media outlets with their own agenda when it comes to covering military matters. We saw much of this during the heat of battle in Iraq. During that time, the media did the best they could to downplay the good things happening in the Middle East and focus on the negative events. Even coverage of Guard deployments for events such as Hurricane Katrina will be covered according to a network or reporter's point of view. For example, Guard coverage during Katrina often focused on overextended forces due to troops serving in Iraq.

The media almost always has an agenda. And whatever that agenda is, you must be very careful if you are approached by the media about National Guard business. If the media outlet or reporter happens to be anti-military or does not support a particular mission, they will look for an unhappy Guard spouse and put them in front of the cameras. They may want to stereotype all Guard families in a particular way and will look for people who fit their point of view.

I don't think there is anything lower than taking advantage of military families when they are feeling frustrated or lonely, and I always feel bad when a military family member does a media interview unprepared. I have heard of newspapers calling FRG leaders to find out if they know anything about casualties that have not been officially announced yet. I mean, how low can you go?

I had some experience with the media while publicizing my first book. What I learned is that you must measure your words very carefully when you are dealing with any type of media outlet. I have been interviewed on radio programs, magazines, newspapers, and on television. And I always take a deep breath when I see the final product. Sometimes I wince when something that I have said was conveniently taken out of context. Or if I say something that I think is funny and it just comes out sounding glib or stupid.

What I realized is that many of the people who we see interviewed on "Good Morning America" or CNN have handlers who are paid thousands of dollars to provide sound bites and media coaching. Our military spokespeople are highly-trained in public affairs. That is why these people are able to sound polished and get their message across.

There is an easy way to avoid worrying about this: don't do any

Strong Bonds

Strong Bonds is a unit-based, chaplain-led program which assists commanders in strengthening army families. The program is conducted in an offsite retreat format and focuses on strengthening communication skills. When the program first launched, it primarily focused on couples post-deployment. It was so well-received that it is now offered to single soldiers, married couples, and families both pre and post-deployment.
www.strongbonds.org

media interviews. If you are considering doing an interview, even with a small local outlet that you are pretty sure will put a positive spin on the piece, please get in touch with your state's Guard Public Affairs Office. Even if you are approached by a writer or editor you know, you should still check with Public Affairs. You can get their contact information on your Guard organization website or by getting in touch with your FAC.

Don't Just Survive—Thrive!

You have a choice to make: you can spend a deployment feeling sorry for yourself or you can actually figure out a way to be happy. It sounds harsh. But it is true. And it seems like an easy choice to me. Control what you can control. You can't control the timing or length of deployment. But you can control how you choose to deal with it. Tell yourself that if you can get through deployment, you can do anything. And you can. Active Army wives have known this for a long time, because one-year unaccompanied tours were a part of Army life. Now Guard spouses are learning it too. When I would get really down, I would remind myself that there were people who were a lot worse off than me. There were moms with four or five kids trying to juggle everything at once. There were people with real crises to deal with such as a financial emergency or fire. And, of course, there were the people who will never see their Soldiers again. When I thought about things through that perspective, it made my Sunday blues seem pretty manageable. While my husband was deployed to Cuba, and after a month of lonely nights, I decided that I needed a long-term challenge. I decided to write a book and spent many nights hunched over my computer, writing away. I also spent a lot of fun lunches with my co-workers brainstorming ideas for the book. And guess what? I got so wrapped up in what I was doing that I actually started to feel better. I had something positive and interesting to keep me occupied. And I had something other than Jon's deployment to discuss with my friends.

When Jon was deployed for Hurricane Katrina for a month, I decided to complete a long-forgotten stage play that I had started writing in 1996! I dusted it off and made a little bit of progress on it every evening and when the kids where in preschool. By the time he returned, it was done. Quite an accomplishment (if I do say so myself). I also decided to take on some major projects around the house. My sister Sheila and her husband Todd rented scaffolding and we painted the entire first floor of my home. Sixteen foot vaulted ceilings and all! I also painted my two-story fireplace. Every night, I would sit at my computer writing and glance down at the fireplace (if you have ever painted brick, you know that it takes forever) and wonder if I would ever finish the project. My goal was to do five rows a night until it was completed. And you know what? I did it. When Jon came home on leave, he was blown away. I was so proud and I know he was too. And every time I look at my ice blue walls and gray fireplace, I am reminded that I not only survived, I thrived.

In addition to caring for her two young daughters while her husband Ed was in Iraq, my good friend Andrea stripped, sanded, primed, and painted the woodwork in her 65-year old Savannah house. She says, "I only have one thing to say to spouses of deployed Soldiers and it is something that I reiterate time and time again: find something to do that keeps you busy and gets you out of bed every day. That may mean a volunteer position in your local community, a home remodeling project, an active position in your FRG, involvement with a church group, or taking a class at the local college or a gym. If you are busy, you don't have time to sit around and worry, stress, complain, or feel lonely." Andrea was an old pro by the time Ed deployed to Afghanistan in 2009.

I could share a hundred examples of military spouses taking on big, bold initiatives when their Soldiers are away. But you get the idea. Even when their Soldiers are home, most of my fellow Guard wives have already started their next list for the next deployment. We are a resilient bunch. We are always ready because we have to be. What does your list include? If you don't have one, it is never too late. I like measurable goals. My next list includes taking Pilates, learning how to sew slipcovers, and volunteering at an animal shelter. And, who knows . . . I may even have another book in me.

Wrap Up

- If you are anticipating a deployment, or are in the middle of one, I encourage you to get online, pick up the phone, and start asking questions. Whatever issue you have, there are people to help you find the support you need.
- When it comes to long-term deployment, your first line of defense is your Family Readiness Group and Family Assistance Center. They can get you the information you need to deal with specific issues and challenges.

- Military OneSource www.militaryonesource.com is filled with excellent information about deployment. The website is updated frequently and it contains the latest and greatest information. The website has a special portal for National Guard family members. If you want to talk to somebody directly, Military OneSource has a 24/7 toll-free number set up for military families.
- Right now–today–start thinking about forming a Personal Assistance League (PAL) to support you during deployments.
- Find a Mother Hen to do the asking for you and anticipate what your needs will be. Make a list of friends and family members who want to help you during deployment. Give them to your Mother Hen.
- Identify the other core resources that you will need: The Dragon Slayer and Nanny 911. Understand that you are living a new normal. Figure out a new way to track time and identify your most vulnerable moments. Let your PAL help you through.
- Use smaller activations to test your plan. Even if your Soldier isn't deployed now, someone else in the Guard family needs your help. Train with them so you know what to expect when your turn comes around. Ultimately, YOU are responsible for getting through deployment. Control what you can control–yourself. Keep your chin up and stay busy. Don't just survive, THRIVE.

Notes

The contents of this book were primarily gathered from friends, acquaintances, and past experiences. There weren't any resources used except for the websites I alluded to in the text.

To make it easier for you, the reader, to view these websites, I have included a list of them here. They are listed in alphabetical order. All of them were active at the time of the publication of this book, however, please be aware that some of them may no longer be available in the future. If the website URL changes, chances are the organization itself has not and you might be able to Google the organization itself. Page numbers refer to the page in which the website is found in the text of this book.

Army G-1 Military Retirement System, page 109
      www.armyg1.army.mil
Army Morale, Welfare and Recreation, page 118
      www.armymwr.com
      www.capehenryinn.com
      www.EdelweissLodgeandResort.com
      www.ShadesofGreen.org
      www.halekoa.com
      www.dragonhilllodge.com
Army Pay, page 108
      https://mypay.dfas.mil
Army Recruiting website, page 32
      www.goarmy.com
Army Retirees Soldiers', Sailors', Marines', Coast Guard, and Airmen's Club
      of New York City, page 119
      www.ssmaclub.org
      centralreservations@redstone.army.mil
Chaplain led programs, page 202
      www.strongbonds.org
Commissary Stores, page 118
      www.commissaries.com
Common Access Card, page 107
      www.cac.mil
Email services, page 135
      www.Mailchimp.com
Enlisted Association of the National Guard of the United States, page 171
      www.eangus.org
Family Readiness Group, page 130, 131
      www.armyfrg.org
Medals, how to wear them and where to purchase, page 70
      www.ezrackbuilder.com
      www.USAMilitaryMedals.com
Military Information source, page 115
      www.military.com
Military Bonus Program, page 116